finding the
inner you

BARRON'S

finding the
inner you

how well do **you** know **yourself**?

Karen Sullivan

introduction **Dr. John Church**

BARRON'S

First edition for the United States,
its territories and dependencies,
and Canada published in 2003 by Barron's
Educational Series, Inc.

Conceived and created by
Axis Publishing Limited
8c Accommodation Road
London NW11 8ED
www.axispublishing.co.uk

finding the **inner you**
contents

Creative Director: Siân Keogh
Editorial Director: Brian Burns
Designer: Sean Keogh
Project Editor: Madeleine Jennings
Production Manager: Sue Bayliss
Production Controller: Juliet Brown

All inquiries should be addressed to:
Barron's Educational Series, Inc.
250 Wireless Boulevard
Hauppauge, New York 11788
www.barronseduc.com

ISBN 0–7641–2270–5

Library of Congress Catalog Card No.:
2001099942

Printed in Germany

9 8 7 6 5 4 3 2 1

More than ever before, we are leading busy and stressful lives. At times, this makes us feel as

though we are unable to cope. The pressures of modern living have made it difficult for us to take

introduction

time out to reflect, relax, and recuperate.

Finding the Inner You *has been conceived for*

everyone who is seeking ways to overcome difficulties they are facing in their lives. It provides

advice on redressing the balance between work and home life, and offers suggestions for finding

self-fulfilment and developing a healthy level of self-esteem. It also gives clear instructions for

performing simple relaxation and meditation techniques, and advises on ways to improve

interpersonal communication and general psychological well-being.

a voyage of
self-exploration and discovery

By adopting the recommendations in this book—many of which are tried-and-tested sound psychological techniques—it is possible to develop into a person you like, admire, and with whom you are very happy to be best friends.

Finding the Inner You *is a voyage of self-exploration and discovery, so different people will find that different sections of the book may suit them more than others. I recommend that you read the book through several times, as this will make it easier for you to consider the plan you need to undertake that best suits your personality and lifestyle.*

In today's society, it is very important to give yourself permission to relax and change. Allowing yourself the time to read ***Finding the Inner You*** *will be the first step.*

Dr. John Church
Chartered Clinical and Counseling Consultant Psychologist
Cognitive Behavioral Psychotherapist

right here right now

The price of a busy lifestyle in a 24/7 society is the loss of self-awareness. Unconsciously—and perhaps even consciously—we push away our thoughts, and determine our identities through our actions rather than our self-beliefs, through reactions rather than instincts, through habit rather than self-understanding. We become the sum of our achievements or failures, and we define ourselves through other people's eyes.

Our unique and defining characteristics—our animating energies—become mass-produced. We do what everyone else does, and we become wary of looking beneath the surface of our day-to-day lives for fear of what we may find. But self-discovery is the journey toward self-awareness and self-acceptance. This journey begins with a mission to understand ourselves, to clear away the debris that masks our real thoughts, true beliefs, and honest opinions.

The confidence to be yourself already exists. Use the exercises in this chapter to look within and find it. You will discover exactly where you are now. Better still, you'll see your own potential to change.

being distracted

Stress is not a novel concept, but it is, unfortunately, a defining feature of our modern age. We are tired, under the weather, and working either at fever pitch or half mast. The way we cope with this situation is by acting rather than being. If we stop, there's a danger of crashing spectacularly, and if we examine our lives too deeply, we are most likely to be worried by what we find there.

Most of us choose to cushion ourselves against self-awareness by setting up a series of distractions that keep us from looking within. The reasons for this are multifold, but the simplest one is that many of us present ourselves to the world in a way that is not a true reflection of what we are or what we feel within. We may be ashamed of some of our own personal characteristics, or we may be held back by self-beliefs that were created for us by others when we were children. We may also feel profoundly discontent with our lives, and may think that keeping up appearances is one way to ensure that the balls are kept in the air. Most importantly, we are likely to feel that others won't respect, like, or admire us if they saw what really lurked beneath the surface. And the reason for this belief is that we do not actually respect, like, or admire ourselves.

Days are busy with work, family, and friends. Evenings are filled with the gym, the Internet, television, music, books, newspapers, and social activities. The average day has no scheduled "down" time, and most of us avoid being alone with ourselves and our thoughts—at all costs. This

may not be a conscious activity, but consider this: When was the last time you sat, alone, and simply entertained your own thoughts—or let them entertain you?

Distractions take the place of positive interaction with ourselves, but they also take the place of meaningful discourse with others—genuine, uplifting, and inspiring communication with friends, family, and colleagues that can help us to see who we are, that encourages us to probe beneath the face we present to the outside world. If you let that face slip a little, what would you find there?

preoccupations

We can kid ourselves into believing that we don't mind being alone, that we enjoy our own company because we spend time alone all the time. But how many of those hours are filled by distractions? How often are we preoccupied?

Television is the most common way to fill our leisure hours and, according to surveys compiled by the TV-Turnoff Network in Washington, D.C., the average person in the U.S. watches over four hours of television a day. Ninety eight percent of households have at least one television (41 percent of households have more than three), and in an average U.S. home, the TV is switched on for 7 hours and 40 minutes each day.

Computers and the Internet are fast catching up on television as a prime leisure activity but, looking at the research, it appears that while we are watching slightly less television, we are filling that time—and about an hour or so extra per day—on the Internet.

You may not be a television watcher, but chances are your time is filled with other distractions, such as reading. How often have you "lost yourself" in a book or magazine? A more noble pursuit than television perhaps, reading still presents an escape from daily life, and from our thoughts.

Think about the other things with which you choose to fill your leisure hours—radios, games consoles, studying, talking on the telephone, reading the paper or a magazine, flipping through catalogs, socializing, exercising with friends or in a group, sending and reading Emails, chat rooms, playing games, and so on. How many of your pursuits are solitary and silent? Even exercising, cooking, or cleaning the house tends to be accompanied by the ubiquitous television or radio in the background.

quick-fix relaxation

Alcohol imbues us with an instant sense of relaxation and well-being, but it also has the ability to obliterate our thoughts, and to shield us from things that are too painful or difficult to consider. It's much easier to drown out a bad day or an overwhelming sense of dissatisfaction than it is to face the possibility that all is not well. Look at the reasons why you have a drink, and consider the fact that it may have something to do with a reluctance to face what's really going on inside.

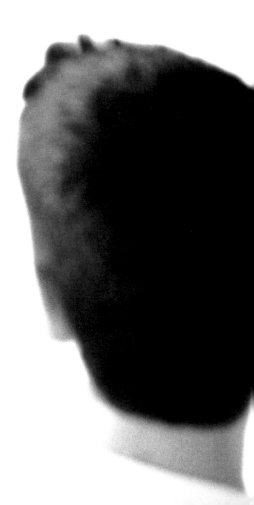

losing the distractions

In order to learn to be alone, and to enjoy your own company, you need to get to know yourself. Distractions take the place of interaction with yourself and your thoughts, so the first thing you need to do is to lose them.

Consider this scenario: You've met an interesting man or woman at a party, and you'd like to get to know them a little better. Would you choose a busy restaurant, with music blaring and the television on in a corner? Would you sit and read quietly while they were talking? Would you meet up in a gym with a trainer shouting out instructions? The answer is, obviously, no.

But the reality is that this is what we do to ourselves. We do not give ourselves the attention, time, and peace we need to come to terms with who we are, what we are, and where we are going. We can't get to know ourselves when interaction is drowned out or silenced.

what is your distraction?

The best place to begin is to record your average day in 30-minute segments. Note the activity you were undertaking, and whether or not you were alone and silent.

In the following scenario, the day has been completely filled by activities that preclude introspective moments, and time alone with thoughts. Obviously your own day might be dramatically different, but it's worth undertaking this exercise to see exactly where your distractions lie.

your day might look something like this:

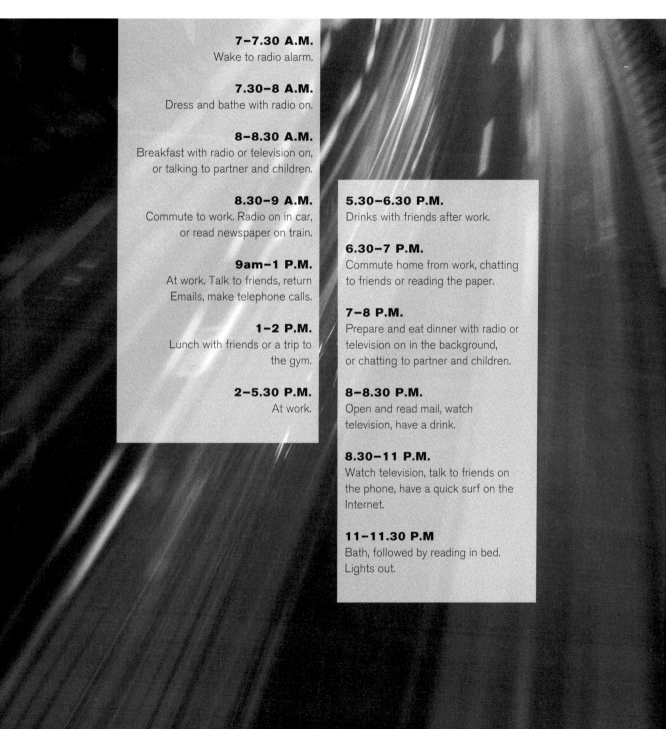

7–7.30 A.M.
Wake to radio alarm.

7.30–8 A.M.
Dress and bathe with radio on.

8–8.30 A.M.
Breakfast with radio or television on,
or talking to partner and children.

8.30–9 A.M.
Commute to work. Radio on in car,
or read newspaper on train.

9am–1 P.M.
At work. Talk to friends, return
Emails, make telephone calls.

1–2 P.M.
Lunch with friends or a trip to
the gym.

2–5.30 P.M.
At work.

5.30–6.30 P.M.
Drinks with friends after work.

6.30–7 P.M.
Commute home from work, chatting
to friends or reading the paper.

7–8 P.M.
Prepare and eat dinner with radio or
television on in the background,
or chatting to partner and children.

8–8.30 P.M.
Open and read mail, watch
television, have a drink.

8.30–11 P.M.
Watch television, talk to friends on
the phone, have a quick surf on the
Internet.

11–11.30 P.M
Bath, followed by reading in bed.
Lights out.

Don't be fooled into thinking that relaxing activities represent "down" time. If you aren't alone with your thoughts, you'll never get to know yourself and you'll never learn to be comfortable with who you are—or make the changes necessary to be yourself.

Once you have completed the previous exercise to discover the distractions you use throughout the day, make a list and choose two or three that you can drop right away: The newspaper or radio on the way to work, for example, or the television for an hour every evening. What's more, look at your day and see where you can carve an hour of free time to allow for introspection.

You may find it difficult to let go of distractions that have become comforts and habits upon which you have come to rely. You may feel bored and agitated on your own, and feel the need for stimulation. This is normal. One of the effects of our busy lifestyles is that we seek constant stimulation in order to keep adrenaline flowing. When we allow ourselves to relax, we tend to crash, or become bored and depressed. Busy lifestyles are addictive, and you will have to wean yourself from your fixes in order to experience the profound relaxation necessary to health and well-being on every level.

feng shui your mind

Most of us are adept at silencing thoughts that do not relate to specific matters, viewing them simply as tools in the decision-making process. But thoughts can be turned within to become tools for self-exploration and understanding. What's more, they can become friends.

In China, the lunar New Year is celebrated loudly with drums, cymbals, and firecrackers to drive out the old energies and welcome in the new. You can do the same with your thoughts. Turn on some loud and happy music, and crank up the volume! Clear your mind of any associations this music has for you, and let it just flow through your body. When you feel mental clutter building up, this is a good trick to clear it out. Do it once a week.

Next, find a place without distractions. Choose somewhere quiet, where you feel peaceful. Sit in a comfy chair or lie down. You may wish to light a candle, to focus your mind and add ambience to your surroundings.

Consciously clear your mind of all thoughts. It helps to visualize a white light or a clear, empty space. Focus on this. When thoughts enter your head, acknowledge them, and let them go. Watch them pass, but don't let them interrupt or intrude. If you find it difficult to carry on, focus on the candle or another item in the room, and begin again. It takes practice to learn the art of peace, but it will eventually provide you with a deep, almost hypnotic sense of relaxation that leaves your mind open to suggestion and change. More than that, however, it teaches you to watch your thoughts and to evaluate them from a distance. This type of passive and detached approach to thinking allows you to be analytical without fearing the repercussions.

As you watch your thoughts pass by, idly consider them. Are there any that make you nervous, or that frighten you? Are there thoughts that you instinctively want to suppress?

When you've finished this exercise, get a pen and paper and write down the thoughts that caused you to feel concern. Examine them and realize that they too can be let go. Try to practice this exercise every day, until you feel comfortable with the process.

In the next chapter we will examine the concept of self-image and how our experiences create our view of ourselves. But before you can work out where you are in life, you need to take an honest look at who you are, and become comfortable with the process of self-analysis.

who are you?

Being at home with your thought processes is the first step. In the previous exercise you learned how to watch your thoughts and to accept them. Let's take that one step further.

In a quiet place where you will not be disturbed, sit down with a pen and piece of paper. Clear your mind of any worries or concerns, then ask yourself, "Who am I?" For this exercise to be useful, you need to rely on instinct and subconscious thoughts, so write down the first words that enter your mind. Do not analyze what comes out, just write it down. This exercise is known as "free association." Any defining characteristics that spring to mind are all equally relevant in the context of free association.

Next, ask yourself the following question, "How would I describe myself?" Again, write down any words that immediately come to mind, for example, sad, funny, lonely, outgoing, nervous, pretty, handsome, confident, gregarious, shy. Once again, don't think about it too much, just write down anything that springs to mind. These instant observations will form the basis of your self-portrait.

On another sheet of paper, make two columns and divide your words into what you consider to be positive and negative attributes. For example, you might consider your shyness to be negative, so put it in the negative column. You might look at some and think they are not strictly accurate but, for the purposes of this exercise, it is all relevant. Put this list away somewhere safe—it will be used later as a point of comparison. You've now taken the first step toward acknowledging your view of yourself.

self-awareness

When we focus on ourselves, we develop our spiritual awareness. We become self-aware. We emanate peace, and the negative emotions and energies of others cannot touch us. The ego—that selfish, fearful, dominating part of our psyche—cannot survive in a state of true self-awareness. When we are at peace—when we know ourselves—we will no longer feel any need to judge, attack, criticize, or control. Fear of others dissolves in the knowledge that we are at one with them, even if they are not aware themselves.

the happiness factor

Many of us believe that feeling good—experiencing a complete sense of well-being—is a luxury. After all, everyone is busy. Work and other pressures take their toll, and it's unlikely that anyone feels complete satisfaction when we live our lives in the throes of the rat race. For this reason, we often neglect our own sense of happiness.

As probably the wealthiest and most financially secure generation in history, it follows that we should also be the happiest. We have jobs, homes, and possessions—lots of them. The majority of us have money to buy far more than the basic necessities of life, and are the proud owners of what would once have been considered luxury possessions. But has this new wealth brought us happiness?

The answer is a simple no. Most research confirms that money is a key factor in happiness—at least until people have reached a certain level of affluence. Beyond that point, its importance falls away, at different rates for different people. But there is also research that shows a more worrying trend. In many countries it seems that, since the 1970s, increased wealth has led to a decline in the public's sense of overall well-being and happiness.

There are many reasons for this trend, but part of the problem is that our growing dependence on consumption brings with it major social problems. We put time and energy into earning to buy and consume, which we might otherwise put into our families, neighborhoods, and communities. More importantly, we have lost time for ourselves, for any kind of meaningful self-interaction.

"About 50 percent of the entire working population are unhappy in their jobs, and as many as 90 percent may be spending much of their time and energy in work that brings them no closer to their goals in life.

Although there are large variations between developed nations in relation to how happy they say they are, the explanation is not differences in wealth.

The well-being of three of the richest nations—Germany, Japan, and the U.S.—is less than that of many poorer developed nations, such as Ireland, Finland, and Australia. Furthermore, the surveys have consistently found little change over time, despite increases in wealth. The U.S., for example, is much richer than in the mid-1900s, yet only about the same numbers say they are happy today as compared to then. Even more dramatically, the Japanese real per capita income increased fivefold between 1958 and 1987 without any change in the amount of reported well-being. Within developed nations, it seems fair to conclude that raising the incomes of all does not necessarily increase the happiness of all.

It's no coincidence that an increasing collective unhappiness has coincided with the growth of the "distraction industry." With less time for ourselves, we pour money into widescreen TVs, expensive entertainment consoles, evenings out, magazine subscriptions, gym memberships, parties, wine, and other fun. But all of this involves living outside the self, outside our minds. Our failure to acknowledge and accept our own identities is one of the main reasons for our collective unhappiness. This unhappiness has also corresponded to a boom in the personal development industry. Dangerously, we are led to believe that to experience happiness, we have to change ourselves and create a better persona.

About 75 percent of those who consult psychiatrists are experiencing problems that can be traced to a lack of job satisfaction." World Health Organisation, 2000.

True, genuine happiness, however, is something much more profound. It is understanding and accepting any weaknesses and shortcomings, and celebrating our individual strengths and successes. It means being comfortable in our own skins, and liking ourselves for what we are, underneath the layers of different identities the years have cast upon us. It means having the confidence and courage to be who we really are.

how happy are you?

Full lives, relationships, work achievements, parenting, leisure pursuits, and holidays all represent a certain level of contentment that can be measured. When we feel unhappy, we blame our jobs, our personal relationships, lack of time, and other vague or specific incidents.

But, just as true happiness needs to be measured from within, it takes a great deal of courage to admit that discontent has its roots in self-identity. We cannot experience real satisfaction, and make a success of our lives, if the foundations of our self-image are faulty. Profoundly happy people are those who have the self-confidence that springs from a strong sense of identity, and who can accept themselves for what they are.

Ultimately, when all is stripped away from our lives, we have only ourselves. If we are unhappy with who we are, then we will never experience genuine contentment.

happiness cannot be measured easily,
but it can be gauged

complete the following questionnaire, ranking your answers on a scale of 1 to 10.

1 How often do you feel intense pleasure?
(Rarely) 1 2 3 4 5 6 7 8 9 10 (Daily)

2 How often do these feelings of pleasure last when they occur?
(Seconds) 1 2 3 4 5 6 7 8 9 10 (Days)

3 Are you afraid of feeling intense pleasure (particularly in the context of great emotional experiences, such as being in love)?
(Frightened) 1 2 3 4 5 6 7 8 9 10 (Not afraid)

4 How often do you experience a feeling of well-being and contentment?
(Never) 1 2 3 4 5 6 7 8 9 10 (Several times a day)

5 When you experience feelings of well-being, do you sometimes act in ways that destroy it?
(Always) 1 2 3 4 5 6 7 8 9 10 (Never)

6 When you have experienced pleasure and a sense of well-being, do you feel guilty, depressed, or anxious?
(Always) 1 2 3 4 5 6 7 8 9 10 (Never)

7 Are you concerned that you will never experience pure happiness and contentment in the future?
(Very worried) 1 2 3 4 5 6 7 8 9 10 (Not worried)

8 Do you have strong hopes for the future?
(Very weak) 1 2 3 4 5 6 7 8 9 10 (Very strong)

9 Do you prefer to keep things harmonious with other people rather than please yourself?
(Yes) 1 2 3 4 5 6 7 8 9 10 (No)

10 Do you find it difficult to express your needs and feelings toward other people?
(Yes) 1 2 3 4 5 6 7 8 9 10 (No)

11 Do you look after your physical health (through diet, exercise, sleep, lifestyle)?
(No) 1 2 3 4 5 6 7 8 9 10 (Yes)

12 Are you in good physical health?
(Poor) 1 2 3 4 5 6 7 8 9 10 (Excellent)

13 Do you smile or show delight easily?
(Rarely) 1 2 3 4 5 6 7 8 9 10 (Very easily)

14 Do you laugh a lot?
(Rarely) 1 2 3 4 5 6 7 8 9 10 (Several times a day)

15 Do you have a high opinion of yourself?
(Very low) 1 2 3 4 5 6 7 8 9 10 (Very high)

16 Do you feel in control of your life?
(Not at all) 1 2 3 4 5 6 7 8 9 10 (Definitely)

17 Do you arrange your daily life so that you have time to relax?
(No) 1 2 3 4 5 6 7 8 9 10 (Yes)

18 Do you feel pressured by your daily life and experience symptoms of stress (such as headaches, irritability, mood swings, digestive problems, trouble sleeping, fatigue, and anxiety)?
(Pressured) 1 2 3 4 5 6 7 8 9 10 (Not at all)

19 Do you have a close group of friends, a partner, or family that you can rely on?

(No) 1 2 3 4 5 6 7 8 9 10 (Yes)

20 Do you have a friend, partner, or family with whom you feel you can always be yourself, regardless of the consequences?

(No) 1 2 3 4 5 6 7 8 9 10 (Yes)

21 Do you push yourself too hard (to be a good parent, good at sports, a success at work)?

(Always) 1 2 3 4 5 6 7 8 9 10 (Never)

22 Are you reluctant to take on new challenges for fear of failure?

(Always) 1 2 3 4 5 6 7 8 9 10 (Never)

23 Do you become extremely upset if you are criticized or corrected?

(Always) 1 2 3 4 5 6 7 8 9 10 (Never)

24 Are you overly critical of others?

(Always) 1 2 3 4 5 6 7 8 9 10 (Never)

25 Do you need continual approval?

(Always) 1 2 3 4 5 6 7 8 9 10 (Never)

26 Do you try too hard to please people?

(Always) 1 2 3 4 5 6 7 8 9 10 (Never)

27 Are you impatient and unappreciative?

(Always) 1 2 3 4 5 6 7 8 9 10 (Never)

28 Do you find it difficult to give yourself a break—a day off or a few hours of self-nurturing?

(Yes) 1 2 3 4 5 6 7 8 9 10 (No)

29 Do you cling to relationships or experiences that make you feel happy?

(Always) 1 2 3 4 5 6 7 8 9 10 (Never)

30 How much of your life would you consider to be fun?

(Very little) 1 2 3 4 5 6 7 8 9 10 (Most of it)

scoring

Add up your numbers and divide the total by 30.

0-4

Any score below five indicates fairly profound dissatisfaction and unhappiness. Look closely at your answers. Why are you finding it difficult to commit to happiness and, most importantly, to yourself?

5-6

Scores between five and seven indicate a low happiness quotient. You aren't experiencing everything that life has to offer. Are you allowing yourself to?

7-8

Scores between seven and nine show promise, but room for improvement. You are holding back in many areas of your life, and you aren't completely sure of yourself. Ask yourself why.

9-10

If you scored nine or ten, relax and enjoy! You are in touch with yourself, and you are experiencing the pleasures of life.

what does happiness mean?

The nature of the questions in this quiz makes it fairly clear that happiness is intrinsically linked to self-esteem and self-confidence. When we are competitive, needy, demanding, unappreciative, overly driven, anxious and unrelaxed, making little time for ourselves, failing to look after ourselves in an emotional and physical context, and showing little sign of pleasure, we lack self-respect. Respect is the cornerstone of love—both of ourselves and of others.

Throughout this book, we will explore the concepts of self-esteem, self-respect, and self-acceptance. These are all crucial to happiness, contentment, fulfilment, satisfaction, and, ultimately, success in all areas of our lives, from relationships through to careers. The beginning point, however, is self-understanding.

You will now have an idea of how you view yourself—if you are profoundly happy, chances are that you also have a strong self-image; if you have scored low on the happiness stakes, there is work to be done. Let's start by practicing being on your own.

a little space

Finding an appropriate space in your home is essential for experiencing solitude and all of its benefits. Have a good look around you—is there any place in your home where you can relax without distractions?

good book, or that night out. At first, you may feel uncomfortable being alone with just your thoughts, but with practice, you'll soon be able to turn yourself inward and enjoy the company of your thoughts wherever you are—on the train, on the way to work, on the treadmill at the gym, in the bath, or even at your desk during quiet periods at work. To begin with, though, you need to make time to shut yourself away in your chosen sanctuary.

Unfinished work, unironed clothing, unanswered correspondence, even untended partners and children will all distract you from spending time alone and getting to know yourself. External clutter not only drains energy, it also creates internal clutter, which makes thinking nearly impossible. No one can turn their thoughts inward if they are distracted by unfinished business.

Make it a priority to clear a space for yourself, where nothing will divert you from the job at hand. Open a window and let fresh air sweep away stale energy. Let in the daylight! Your chosen sanctuary should be quiet, relaxing, and out of bounds to the rest of the household.

time for space

Most of us argue that time is at a premium, that there simply aren't enough hours in the day to carve out more. But remember the old adage: You always find time for the things you put first. For once, put yourself first. The best way to find time is to replace your "distraction time" with quiet time. Give up the surf on the Internet, the

If you really can't find 30 minutes or an hour in the day, set your alarm a little earlier and create time then. The house will be quieter and more conducive to introspection. Allocate time in your diary for "you," and promise yourself that these appointments are unbreakable, no matter what.

necessary natural light

The endocrine system, which is governed by the pituitary and pineal glands, requires light in order to function properly. These glands control the release of hormones into the body that are closely linked to moods and emotions. Many holistic practitioners also believe that natural light (living light) is necessary for the soul or "spirit." Like plants, humans need natural, living light in order to thrive and to grow. Whether this works on an energy level or not is unclear, but we do know that children who live in an environment with little light fail to thrive. Many therapists believe that we absorb energy (or chi) from light and air, and that failure to get this energy results in an impaired sense of well-being.

the art of meditation

Meditation is a tool to make us aware of the peace within us, the forgotten place that the outside world cannot touch or influence. The word meditation comes from the Latin "moderi," meaning to heal. Healing erases pain, hurt and suffering, and helps to draw us away from the costume of our body to the peace within. Pain, hurt, and suffering cannot touch us when we heal, and when we are healed, we are strong enough to live our lives as ourselves, resisting the influences around us.

begin a meditation

Go to your own quiet space. Make sure it is cool and lit naturally. Give yourself a few moments to wind down. Sit comfortably and shut your eyes. Let your breathing become deep and rhythmic. Let your thoughts flow.

Grab the first thought that goes past. Maybe you are concerned about meeting a deadline. Hold that thought and consider what it tells you about yourself. Are you afraid? Are you worried? Then, let the thought go.

Your next thought may be about the financial implications of missing a deadline. Why are you afraid? What can a feeling of peace do to that emotion? Follow the path of your thoughts as they guide you to the quiet calm of your inner spirit. What do you feel there?

Peace? A moment of reckoning? A crystal-clear idea of where to go next? Or do you just feel a sense of calm? Many people experience an epiphany while meditating. Others simply experience gentle insights.

As you continue with your thoughts, imagine yourself exploring all the rooms of your mind, washing each one clean with a burst of bright white light. Let your thoughts enter your head, and then let them go again on the waves of white light. Let your thoughts progress from room to room. Each chamber of the mind offers insight.

Afterward, write your thoughts down in a journal. Treasure them and contemplate them. These thoughts form the foundation of self-knowledge and understanding— freedom from the world around us.

meditation is the tool for expanding your

meditate on color

The symbolism of colors is universal: Red is bold and empowering; green represents renewal and a fresh start; blue is associated with peace and well-being (the Egyptians saw blue as an image of the heavens); and white light embodies wholeness, purity, and spiritual clarity. Visualize a color clearly in your mind's eye. Imagine it as fully as you can in all its depth and richness. Reflect upon its qualities and try to assume those you seek.

mind and maintaining self-awareness

mindful breathing

When Buddha was once asked by a disciple whether there was one particular quality one should cultivate that would best bring one to full awakening, Buddha answered by saying, "Being mindful of breathing."

You do not need to be a Buddhist to see the virtue of this thinking, but it's worth understanding how Buddhism views the self. There is no "god" in Buddhism; rather, it is better described as a philosophy of life. It proposes that the enlightened qualities of humanity exist in each of us, and that we should all seek our own enlightenment and find our own answers to the meaning of life.

Buddhism is founded on the utmost respect for life. We decide for ourselves what is the best course of action, based on our own innate wisdom, which arises and develops through practice. Deep down, what matters is that we feel connected—with others, and the universe, but, most importantly, ourselves.

Buddhism began by encouraging its practitioners to engage in *smrti* (sati) or mindfulness; that is, developing a full consciousness of all about you and within you—whether it is when you are seated in a special posture, or when you are simply going about your daily life.

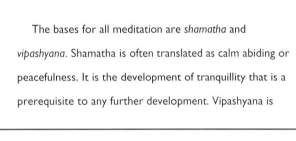

The bases for all meditation are *shamatha* and
vipashyana. Shamatha is often translated as calm abiding or
peacefulness. It is the development of tranquillity that is a
prerequisite to any further development. Vipashyana is

clear seeing or special insight, and involves intuitive
cognition of suffering, impermanence, and egolessness.

I am not Buddhist, but I cannot deny the commonsense
attribute this way of thinking has as a route to happiness,
well-being and, ultimately, peace. Given the nature of our
exhausting and often strife-filled existence, it's reassuring
to know that we can find the answers within.

the most basic form of meditation involves paying

basic meditation techniques

1 Begin by sitting in a simple chair, keeping your back erect if you can. The more traditional postures are the lotus position (sitting on a pillow with each foot on the opposite thigh) or half lotus (one foot on the opposite thigh, the other out in front of the opposite knee). Beginners may find these positions uncomfortable at first.

2 Your head should be upright, but your neck not rigid. Close your eyes or focus them on your hands or on a spot on the ground a couple of feet ahead. Many people find it easier to keep their eyes open during this meditation, for the simple reason that it can lull you into such a deep state of relaxation that you may fall asleep!

3 You can place your hands flat on your thighs, or in the traditional position—palms upward, one hand loosely on the other with thumbs touching—or in any position that feels comfortable.

4 Begin by counting your breaths, on the exhalation, up to ten. Start again at one. If you lose track, simply go back to one again. Your breath should be slow and regular, but not forced or artificially controlled. Just breathe naturally and count.

5 When you are distracted by sounds or other interruptions, acknowledge them, but do not let them disturb your breathing. Do not become attached to them. Just watch them and let them go.

6 You may find this process difficult at first. We are so used to accepting a barrage of thoughts and images that our minds are trained to race constantly. If you find it difficult simply to watch your thoughts, aim to visualize a picture instead. Shut your eyes and imagine a warm, sunny day, with white clouds floating in a gentle breeze in a deep-blue sky. When you experience a thought, mentally attach it to a cloud, name it, and allow it to float away. Do this with every thought you have, counting your breaths as you do so. You will eventually find that your mind calms sufficiently to allow the deep relaxation that breathing creates, and your thoughts will begin to pass quietly of their own accord.

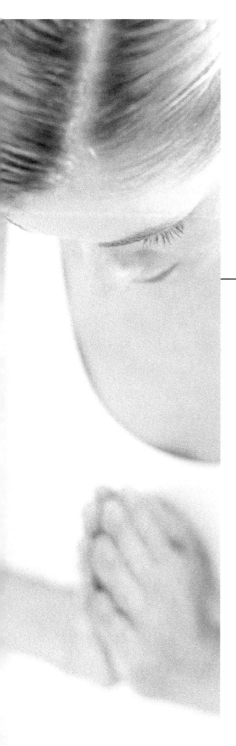

attention to, or being mindful of, your breath

After a few weeks, you may forego the counting and simply breathe. Concentrate on your breath entering you and exiting you. Be as fully aware as possible of the entire process of breathing. Some experts suggest imagining the air entering and exiting lower in your body—about an inch below your navel. The belief is that focusing your mind lower down the body leads to deeper meditation. If this causes you to feel drowsy, focus higher up, around your nostrils or your mouth, for example.

Everyone experiences different things when meditating, and you may find periods of enlightenment, some of boredom, some of a powerful sense of peace, and others that are very emotional. Don't stop and analyze these feelings. Just acknowledge them, then let them go. Continue to breathe. According to Buddhism, the breathing is enlightenment.

being alone

It's not easy being alone. We have busy lives, and tend to fill up all our time—sleeping, preparing and eating meals, organizing social activities, doing domestic chores, seeing families and friends. It's a difficult transition to accepting the lingering peacefulness of solitude, and you may feel discomfort, boredom, or perhaps even fear. Many people confess to feeling agitated, and are desperate for some sort of distraction. If you feel this way, it's very likely that you do not want to confront your existing situation, or come to terms with who you are now. We hide behind distractions, and we often fill our time to avoid having to look within. Soul-searching is a solitary activity, and so is the process of defining yourself.

Your responses to the previous and following exercises show your general state of emotional health—whether you are happy and your self-respect is strong enough to weather criticism from others. The questionnaire on pages 28–29 is designed to gauge happiness, but it also presents critical questions that you must ask yourself and answer honestly. The answers on which you scored the lowest will tell you a great deal about where you are now.

Can you sit comfortably without experiencing agitation or boredom? What are you distractions and when do you use them? When you are alone, how do you feel?

If you've managed to undertake the meditation and relaxation exercises in this chapter, you have taken the first step on the journey toward being your own best friend, and learning to like, respect, and admire yourself. What's more, you've been alone, without distractions. And you may not have even felt the need to go out seeking them. Continue the exercises, daily if you can, as you travel through this book. You've had the first glimpse of what is inside and, whether you like it or not, your own self-image. In the next chapter, we'll find out how you really see yourself, and how to get rid of the things that do not need to be there.

VALUABLE TIME

Before you begin your journey of self-discovery, take time out for assessing yourself and the values by which you live. Examine your life as it is today and reflect honestly on the life you have created. Decide what is worth keeping and what is now worn out. Meditate on these thoughts.

the way you see yourself 2

We tend to see ourselves through the eyes of others, making small changes to our personalities and manners (and mannerisms) in response to others. Humans are canny creatures, and have an underlying need to be liked by others. We unconsciously and constantly adapt ourselves to ensure that we are liked. This process begins in childhood, when we learn to behave in response to labels we are given, expectations our parents have, the way our peers view us, and the minutiae of experiences that cause us to look at ourselves in new ways. Over the years, layers of different traits and identities build up, masking the real person we are beneath. We develop public masks, and end up living up to images that have little to do with who we really are.

Layers are often constructed on preconceptions and misconceptions, becoming barriers to self-knowledge. They also prevent the development of healthy relationships with others because they disguise our true selves. In this chapter, we'll look at ways to discard the outer shell to reveal the person you feel most comfortable being—yourself.

role-playing

Most of us reach a point in our lives where we have achieved a certain degree of visible success—friends, social activities, hobbies, interests, jobs, and families. We manage this by making changes and sacrifices toward becoming a

person capable of playing our part—as a friend, neighbor, squash partner, lover, parent, and worker. But ask yourself this—do any or all of these people view you in the same way? Are you different in the company of various people? Do you feel sometimes that no one really gets a sense of the real you? Do you sometimes feel that you are acting, playing a role that has been predefined by the nature of the interaction?

It's natural to behave differently in different company. We would not, for example, show our more sensitive characteristics to a demanding employer, nor would we allow our children or perhaps our sports partners to see our sensual side. The real issue, however, is that we tend to create roles for ourselves according to what we believe others want from us. Often, we don't just behave in different ways, we become different people. At the office, we play the role of hard-hitting businessman or woman, at home we are the doting parent or disciplinarian, in the company of our friends we are the relaxed, funny drinker.

Role-playing can be exhausting and undermining. We are left with mixed feelings following interactions with others— pleased that we have met expectations and played the part well, but discomfited by the fact that we were not able to be ourselves. What's worse, however, is that after time we tend to believe in the roles we are playing, and adapt our lifestyles and personalities to fulfill them. We lose our sense of identity and no longer even know who we are.

Consider, for example, a woman who has been through a painful divorce and has been left with two young children. She senses that, although her friends and colleagues are

sympathetic, they are unwilling to become too involved, and are slightly uncomfortable with her emotional state. In response to this, she closes down and presents herself as someone who is together, relaxed, dynamic, and unemotional. She throws herself into caring for her children, and receives many complimentary and envious comments about how well she is coping, how she has become Supermom, capable of anything. Pleased with this reaction, she attempts to do more to achieve positive recognition, and becomes a Superwoman in every way. Over time, this role becomes her reality, her identity, and ultimately, a distraction from her true feelings and self.

CHAMELEONS

When we take the expectations of others too much into account—playing out roles they have assigned us—we may find that we lose sense of our true identity.

This is just one clear example of how circumstances and the response of other people can change not only the way we act and communicate, but also how we view ourselves. If we meet with criticism or suspect disapproval, we change to become someone more acceptable. Over time, we accumulate a variety of different roles and begin to lose track of who we are underneath. This is the basis of the "crises" that so many people face in later life, when they are forced to ask themselves, "Who am I?" and "Do I really like what I have become?"

EARNING AFFECTION

A reticent, book-loving boy may have quickly
learned that his sports-mad, macho father didn't
appreciate these particular qualities, and
changed to fit the bill of suitable son.

desperate to please

Many of the roles we play are created in childhood. We learn quickly and instinctively what others expect from us and, ever willing to please, we adapt to become someone who is liked and admired. We may have found that being rebellious, loud, and gregarious did not please a pristine, quiet mother, so developed an alternate persona to please her, or that being accepted by the "in-crowd" at school required a certain attitude and dress sense.

In some cases these roles are carried on through life. In other cases, they are simply built upon as more and more roles are added to the repertoire. You may have friends who still behave in an uncharacteristic way—often completely unwittingly—with their parents and siblings. They slip into roles without thinking because it is the role they have always played in the context of their families.

Throughout our lives we adopt different roles according to what we perceive is expected of us, or what we believe is attractive and acceptable. For example, we take on the role of rebellious, heavy drinker with college friends. Then, when the label of "good fun" is established, we carry on, later forgetting why we began to behave in such a way. We may have been creative and artistic, but got short shrift from our peers or parents, so channeled our energies into playing top athlete or keen academic instead. We played the role, settled into it, then forgot there was ever anything different there to begin with.

what's your role?

If you could choose a few words to describe yourself, what would they be? Dynamic, ambitious, gregarious business person? Fun-loving, sociable singleton? Relaxed earth mom? Take a few moments to write down how you view yourself today and how, perhaps, you feel other people see you. Now look back across your career and your life. What other roles have you played? Consider your first job, your relationships, your years of education, and childhood. Write down the various roles you have played, and when they were played. As you work back, you will see that you have played different roles—and even been different people—at different points in your life. Consider the degree to which the company you kept altered the roles you played. Which of these roles was closest to the real you? Would you feel comfortable playing any of them again? Do you cringe when you look back?

The object of this exercise is to analyze where and how changes were made to your self-perception and self-image during your life. By understanding why and how you changed (job expectations, the demands of a lover, or the prerequisites of a social group), you can begin to accept that some of the things that may have gone wrong in your life—or run off track—were responses to external pressures. All of us change in these circumstances, and you need to know that role-playing doesn't make you weak-willed or shallow; it merely represents changes you made to preserve your own well-being.

Try to remember how you felt playing these roles. Can you remember feelings of duplicitousness, inadequacy, or insecurity? The roles that you played most easily and effortlessly are probably those that are closest to the real you.

the label game

Your parents will have made a direct
impact on your attitude, behavior, and self-image, so it's
worth looking back to the way they labeled you as a child,
and the way you interacted with them.

A child trusts his parents completely. He asks questions about his world, and they are answered. Parents are the all-powerful source of knowledge, and children learn by watching and listening to them. You are told that the sky is blue, that "1, 2, 3" is counting, that shoes go on feet, and night is for sleeping. You are told that cats have kittens, that books are for reading, and that a cow says "moo."

Children believe what they are told, and this belief is validated by the fact that others seem to be in agreement. Grandparents give the same response to a child's questions; his playmates all believe the same thing; his babysitter confirms that cows do say "moo." His trust is complete. Everything that is said to a child will be taken seriously. The problem is, of course, that parents are busy, tired, and often unaware that the little things they say have a profound impact. You may have been called stupid, naughty, bad, spoiled, silly, jealous, dumb, impossible to live with, selfish, self-centered—all sorts of things that slipped out in the course of an argument or in the throes of a chaotic day. When parents become angry, upset, frustrated, busy, or just exhausted, they often say things they don't intend, and it is, of course, the source of much parental guilt.

But these words and throw-away comments can have deep-seated ramifications. Whether you remember it or not, you will have believed your parents. If you were told you were stupid, even in a burst of anger, you will have mentally filed that characteristic away. If you were told you were selfish, you will have believed it. Every negative word that was used to define you will have been taken onboard unconsciously. You may not remember a particular incident, nor will you have been traumatized for life by being called naughty or horrible. Yet, these experiences will have formed faulty bricks in the foundation of your self-image and helped create a negative self-identity. When these descriptions are used repeatedly, they become labels, and labels have a habit of becoming self-fulfilling prophecies.

even positive labels can have a damaging effect on children

Even positive labels can have a damaging effect on children. Although you may have benefited from the praise and good feelings that came with having been consistently labeled "bright," "musical," "good," or "very funny," you may also have acquired a cross to bear—an image that you felt you had to live up to. You may have seen yourself in the light your parents created for you, and worked hard to sustain that image which they enjoyed or made them proud. Much of our identities and the way we view ourselves—our core beliefs—is derived from subtle shifts of behavior made in childhood to fit a positive label, or feelings of inadequacy associated with negative labels. Not surprisingly, at this young age, self-identity becomes cluttered and confused, and we begin to act in ways that we know will please others—a habit that can last a lifetime.

Think back to your childhood. Were you the good one in the family or the black sheep? Were you the bright one, or did you have to struggle? Could you always be relied upon to lift a dark cloud with funny stories and jokes, or were you hard work to have around?

analyzing your labels

Make a list of the characteristics—both negative and positive—that best describe you as a child. Now try to recall any insecurities you had. Do you remember having trouble with peers? Did you have problems communicating

your feelings? Next, talk to a sibling, close childhood friends, and your parents. Ask them to describe the same things. You should uncover two things from this exercise. First of all, you will find that many of the self-beliefs you hold now are not actually accurate. You may have seen yourself as being naughty, gloomy, anxious, overly eager to please, or bad, while none of the recollections of your family and peers corroborate this. In this case, it's likely that a few experiences or throw-away comments caused you to believe something about yourself that simply wasn't true. Secondly, you will find that people remember certain parts of your personality or behavior that were defined by your labels, even though you struggled to shake these off in adulthood. You may find that your parents still think you are the difficult one, even though you have gone on to have healthy relationships and smooth interactions. The struggle against these labels can be frustrating, but it's important to see them as being only that—tags used for classification, not an accurate reflection of your true identity. Consider the labels that bother you the most, and ask yourself: Why? If you were labeled shy, and it became a

burden to bear throughout your life, something against which you have repeatedly fought, ask yourself this: What is wrong with being a shy child? Try to reframe it as a positive label. Try to remember specific experiences that led you to believe something about yourself—an embarrassing performance on stage, for example, that stuck with you for years afterward. Look back on the list of characteristics you've used to describe yourself as a child. How many of them can be applied to you today? Think carefully about this. Do you harbor these labels beneath the surface, act in the opposite way in a continuous attempt to rid yourself of them, or work very hard to fulfill them?

Let's take a practical example. Let's say you were raised by an intolerant father who was a great thinker and a member of the intellectual elite. You struggled in school and, for years, put up with subtle references to your inferiority, inability to think things through, lack of

imagination, inarticulacy—your lack of intelligence. One of two scenarios will have resulted. The first is that you took on board this perception and made it your own. You believed throughout your life that you were intellectually inadequate. As a result, you never pushed yourself down routes that may have been appropriate because you feared further rejection and lacked the self-belief to do so. Chances are you were intelligent—most humans are in some way—but never trusted yourself to show it or use it. The second scenario is that you spent your life trying to prove this label false and set yourself unrelenting standards. You pushed yourself to excel in academic fields that held little or no interest, educated yourself, criticized others for their stupidity, took every opportunity to prove your intelligence to your colleagues and friends, all in an attempt to prove that your father was wrong. Of course, these aren't conscious actions, but they nonetheless define your self-image now, feeding a deep-seated insecurity and lack of self-belief.

Remember, too, that labels can be acquired all throughout our lives, and can be equally difficult to shift. Look back at the labels that you have been given at different points in your life. In essence, these will be the single adjective that people use to describe you. What would yours be? What was it at key points in your life? Do you think you fit the label? Did you ever?

SETTING THE INTERNAL TEMPLATE

Being caught in the throes of a first kiss by a disgusted parent may have made you feel indecent or immoral, and you may have carried this view of yourself into later adult relationships.

do you think you fit the label? did you ever?

peeling the onion

When homeopaths begin to treat patients, they liken the process to peeling an onion. In other words, as each "layer" of ill-health is healed, the next presents itself for healing. Eventually, all layers are worked through until a core of untainted good health and well-being is reached.

Much the same principle can be applied to your journey toward self-awareness and realizing your potential. In order to reach the core of your identity—what you really are, and what you are capable of being—you need to peel back the layers of experience that hide it. Consider it a voyage of self-discovery. This process can be time-consuming and emotional. It also requires honesty, and an ability to forgive yourself and others along the way.

When you strip back your layers, you will inevitably face disturbing recollections of experiences that may have caused you to put up defenses. But beneath the layers, you will also find the person you like most of all—yourself. Self-like is crucial to the process of living—to well-being, successful careers and relationships, and an ability to experience and enjoy life to the fullest.

We started to peel back the layers when we looked at the roles we have played throughout our lives, and at the labels we have acquired. Now we'll take it a step further.

Look back at the characteristics you used to define yourself in chapter one (see page 20).

THE REAL YOU

Your layers represent the barriers you have set up against being yourself, against experiencing true interaction and honest relationships, and realizing genuine success.

get out there and communicate with others

What you need to do now is to get out there and communicate with others. Compare the perception you have of yourself with other people's perception of you. Ask your boss, your children, your friends, family, and neighbors—anyone who will take part—to list your three best and worst characteristics. Try not to be offended if their responses take you by surprise! Write all of them down on a piece of paper, divided into two columns: positive and negative characteristics.

Now compare this list with the list you made yourself. Looking at the positive column first, ask yourself: How many are the same? Of the ones that are the same, did you consider them to be positive features because they are important to other people, make you more likeable, or because they are a key part of the person you are today? Or did you list them because they are features that you genuinely like about yourself?

Consider each description in order, and reflect upon them individually. Make a third list of positive features and, under this, write the positive traits that you actually like about yourself. Then add those that you feel accurately describe the person you are beneath the surface.

Look at the positive features other people mentioned. How many do you feel are accurate? Those that you feel genuinely describe you should be added to your third list, too.

How many of the positive features that other people mentioned are new? Consider each of them carefully. If you feel that they genuinely describe the "real" you, add them to the third list. If you feel that they are characteristics of a role you are playing, or they define a label you have acquired, put a star beside them.

stop and take pleasure in the positive

characteristics attributed to you

As you do this exercise, don't forget to stop and take pleasure in the positive characteristics that others have attributed to you. Even if they are not strictly accurate, they provide food for thought, and for self-liking!

Next, let's look at the negative characteristics. How many of these are the same? Consider them carefully: Are they features of your personality that were developed through a role you were playing? Are they the result of labels given at some point in your life? Put a star beside any that are label- or role-related.

Look at the characteristics remaining. How many of them are accurate? For those that are on target, ask yourself whether they really are negative characteristics, or whether some people might consider them positive. For example, weak-willed could be described as easy-going; shy considered as sensitive and appealing; aggressive perhaps ambitious or determined; and discontent may be nothing more than a springboard to change. Where you can, change the names of your negative qualities to something more positive, and add them to the positive column.

Now consider the following question: Do you think some of your characteristics are negative because other people do? Or are they really parts about yourself that you dislike? Write down the characteristics you consider to be negative because you are viewing yourself through other people's eyes to the third list of negative traits.

For the negative qualities that remain, ask yourself whether they are genuine parts of your personality. If they are, add them to the third list.

analyzing your results

The third list of positive and negative attributes represent the real you, the one lying beneath the layers. As you examine them, remember that everyone has points about themselves that are less than perfect. The object is to learn to like yourself—the whole package, good and bad. We all have friends with features we dislike. Flaws are part of the human makeup, and an important part of our identities.

Just as you accept and make allowances for the shortcomings of your friends and family, allow yourself to embrace and appreciate your own limitations and imperfections. They form part of the real you and are as valid as your good points.

Take time to concentrate on your good points. Remind yourself constantly of their existence, particularly when you are feeling low, or are overwhelmed by shortcomings. Focus particularly on those characteristics described by others. Explore and enhance them further.

The starred entries in your personal inventory represent qualities that have been developed as a part of a role you are playing. They are a feature of a label you are living up to, or are character traits you have acquired as a result of trying to be someone else—a better or different you. These entries also represent the parts of your self-identity that are holding you back.

No one can move forward or interact positively when their self-identity is cluttered. You need to feng shui your self-image before you can realize the strength of what lies beneath. Look at the starred negative characteristics. Work out where they came from, then let them go. Look at the starred positive characteristics. Accept that they played a part in getting you where you are now, but that they are no longer necessary. Work out why they were developed, then do the same thing. Let them go.

It sometimes helps to visualize this exercise. Prepare yourself as if for meditation (see page 34). When your breathing is regular, visualize each characteristic as a layer that is masking the true you lying at the heart. Imagine unpeeling it like an onion, then discarding the peels into a trash can. Do the same with each characteristic, until you are left with just your core. This core represents the person you are going to learn to love—someone who is capable of anything and everything because he or she has the self-confidence, self-belief, self-awareness, and self-love to shine. People will be attracted to you because you embody a sense of being at peace with yourself. Success will come your way because positive energy attracts positive interaction and achievement. Things will become easier because you can make decisions without the confusion of alternate personae, and the need to live up to other people's expectations.

MEDITATE ON IT
Find a quiet, secluded space without any distractions and allocate some time to perform the visualization exercises.

positive interaction

You've now identified the barriers
to becoming the person you are beneath, the "real" you.
As you begin to let go of any preconceptions

you may have about yourself—letting chinks of light into
the personality and character that has been enshrouded in
darkness for so long—you will most likely find that others
begin to respond differently to you.

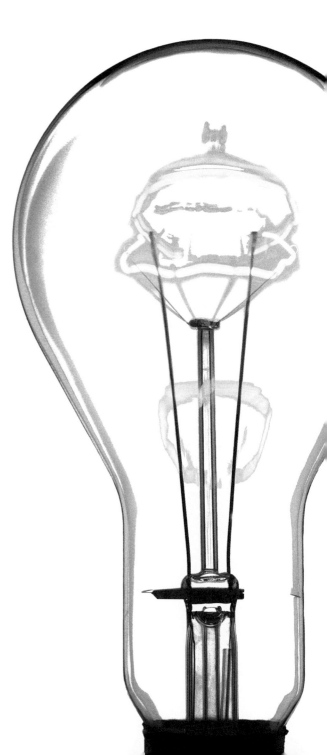

You may discover that people who have never been interested before are drawn to you, and you may find that others are wary of what could be perceived as a

new persona. By being yourself, however, you will be interacting with complete and utter honesty, which precludes distrust on the part of others. People respond to us according to the signals we send out. If we have a negative self-image, we will attract negative comments and negative interactions. If we think little of ourselves, others will undoubtedly respond in kind. No one genuinely respects or admires a person who is unworthy of such attentions. In the past, you may have found that you were the center of envy or admiration because of the skills you acquired as part of a role you were playing. You will also, however, have felt that something was holding you back, that you weren't as successful as you felt you should have been.

That "something" is your negative self-image—and you may not have even known that it was there. Having shed it, however, you will be exuding a new kind of confidence and peace that is—sometimes simply on an unconscious level—attractive to others. And that positive spirit unfailingly garners success in other areas of your life.

In Chapter 5, Communication, we'll explore some of the best methods that you can use to express your new self. For the time being, however, let's simply focus on living as the person you are underneath all your layers. So, when you catch yourself adopting roles or trying to be someone you are not, stop and visualize that layer being peeled away. Let your true spirit shine, and you will soon experience new and positive interactions.

love thee, love thyself

Learn to nurture yourself. Take time to celebrate the positive parts of your character—your strengths, abilities, talents, and uniqueness. Try to consider your negative

characteristics in a new light. What may seem to you a flaw can, in fact, be the very thing that draws others to you. You like others for their unique blend of good and bad, and you must learn to see yourself the same way—as someone who is loveable and worthy, warts and all.

Self-love demands self-respect. When we respect others, we treat them well. You must learn to do the same thing to yourself. Consider the questionnaire back in Chapter 1, How Happy Are You? (see pages 26–31). Many of the questions relate to looking after ourselves—both physically and emotionally. When we feel bad about ourselves, we tend to let ourselves go. We don't eat well, we don't get enough sleep, and we don't take part in life's pleasures. We probably abuse our bodies with more alcohol and cigarettes than before, too. We may also surround ourselves with distractions that prevent us from looking too deeply, or we might care too much for someone that we would normally consider to be unworthy. Emotionally, we may not take a break—to relax, rejuvenate, reflect, and have fun.

We do not seek out and sustain life-enhancing and stimulating interactions with others, or with ourselves. We fail to examine our emotions, and the consequences of this are that we never truly begin to understand why we react the way we do, and we never experience the type of passion that is essential for embracing a fulfilling life.

Many of us have been conditioned to consider self-nurturing to be self-indulgent, hedonistic, lazy, and even narcissistic. In fact, it's anything but. We care for the things that matter most in our lives—our family, children, friends, pets, plants, and we usually enjoy indulging those that matter most to us. Self-indulgence is equally important. It indicates the respect we have for ourselves that is a prerequisite to true self-liking.

do something that feels
absolutely sinful

start now!

Block off time in your diary for yourself, and do something that feels absolutely sinful. Give yourself permission to enjoy treats—they add pleasure to life and help you to make the changes that you want. Replace the habit of self-criticism with the habit of rewarding yourself.

Living in the present, accepting responsibility for problem areas of your life, and taking steps to change them require courage and determination, as well as self-belief, but they are necessary steps if you wish to progress to a more satisfying and healthy lifestyle.

Above all, choose to make changes toward well-being. To do this, you need to clearly identify problem areas, and understand why you practice behaviors that are not conducive to a healthy lifestyle. Many people blame the past or others for their problems. Being overweight, for example, is often attributed to poor eating habits as a child.

Treat yourself as a treasured friend. Spend time in your own company and let your thoughts entertain you. Hold internal dialogues, and watch your imagination take you places where you never thought you'd go. Spend time with yourself because you want to. Appreciate your positive attributes and raise your own self-esteem!

Make those necessary lifestyle changes. Eat well, look after your body, dress in clothes that make you feel comfortable and good about yourself, exercise regularly, and cut down or (even better) cut out the quick-fix relaxation habits, such as smoking and drinking to excess. Take time to look at the stresses in your life, with a view to making radical changes. Look at your life through the eyes of someone else. What advice would you give in response to the question: How can I make changes toward healthy well-being? When you have the answers, put them into action.

understand that mistakes
are part of the learning curve

self-confidence

Building self-confidence takes practice. Learn from your mistakes, and understand that mistakes are part of a learning curve. Silence the voice of self-blame and speak encouragingly to yourself. Be kind to yourself. To build self-esteem, attack those prejudices which led you to undervalue yourself in the first place. Low self-esteem is a

prejudice about oneself—seeing oneself as unworthy or unacceptable. The self-perception is biased or flawed, but a prejudiced person has a hard time seeing it any other way. Learn to acknowledge your qualities rather than discount them. You also need to learn to stifle your inner critic—congratulate yourself instead! See the good in what you have done. Do the best you can, and don't berate yourself for not being perfect at everything. Finally, try to spend time with people who make you feel good about yourself. And be one of those people yourself!

When you are good to yourself, you begin to acquire a new self-respect. With respect comes a healthy sense of pride that precludes others' attempts to unseat you. You will no longer put up with bullying, unkind behavior, being taken advantage of, or disrespected. Your new confidence will become a beacon to success and healthy relationships. In a nutshell, you'll be worthy of exceptional treatment by others simply because you believe yourself to be worthy.

The three-point reward system

1 Choose treats that work for you. Think about the things that you enjoy that give you pleasure, that make you laugh and help you to relax. Read a book, enjoy good company, dine out, watch a classic film, go away for the weekend, have a bubble bath, or spend the night in with a video.

2 Make your system long term. Treat yourself often with things that satisfy you. If having a cigarette, a drink, or a bar of chocolate only perpetuates the search for pleasure, or makes you feel less lonely or better only briefly, they may be the wrong treats for you. Try saving up lots of little treats to have in one indulgent go.

3 Avoid the punishment trap. Do not fall into the trap of serving other people's needs at the expense of your own. Do not make a virtue out of being a martyr. Part of treating yourself right is putting yourself first, and doing things that please you, be it for yourself or for others.

your emotional self

3

Emotional expression is the ultimate form of communication. When we suppress or deny emotion, we are effectively removing the tools that others need to understand, get to know, and like us. But we also deny ourselves the opportunity to make our true selves known, and to free ourselves from the layers of unspent emotional energy that cloud our relationships, both with ourselves and with others.

When we release emotion, we expose ourselves to the world around us. While this can be a frightening concept, it is essential for effective communication and self-understanding. Self-expression is difficult for many of us, but it is a skill that can be acquired. Very soon you will feel at ease with yourself, and learn to value what you have to say and feel.

Emotional expression also opens us up to intuition, to the natural release of energy—both positive and negative—and to self-awareness.

In this chapter, you'll learn how to recognize, accept, and use emotion to change the way you feel about yourself, and to make your true self known to the world around you.

what is emotion?

Modern psychology, as well as ancient Hindu and Buddhist doctrines called Tantra, contend that, rather than mastering our emotions, we should learn to live in equilibrium with them, and use the energy that they give us.

Understanding emotions can be difficult because we are often too close to them to perceive them clearly. Getting some distance from them, and viewing them objectively, is a valuable part of learning to use them profitably. Emotions are so malleable because the basic feelings that underlie them are fuzzy and hard to pin down. With practice, we can easily persuade an emotion to turn into something else. For example, research suggests that boredom, disgust, and loathing are all the same feeling. The only thing that differentiates them is intensity. The same is true of pensiveness, sadness, and grief. Other research has discovered that, often, all we feel is an immense potential to experience an emotion. The one we actually feel is determined by a number of factors, including posture, cultural background, what we are thinking at the time, and, perhaps most importantly, what we are telling ourselves.

What all these findings suggest is that our emotions are largely illusory, and that to find peace we can try to manipulate our bodies, their environments, the sounds we hear, and the colors we look at. This is the basis of many of the therapies—yoga, meditation, color therapy—that many of us use on our quest for peace. More importantly, these findings remind us that we are not slaves to our emotions, no matter how much we may feel so at a given time.

an emotional vocabulary

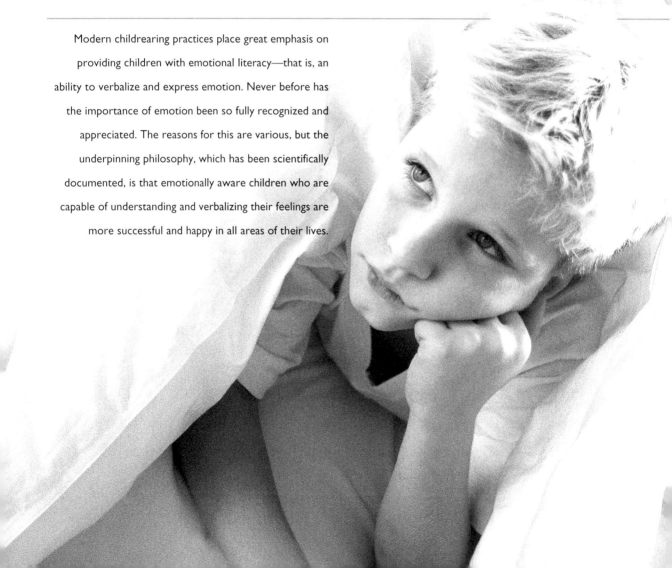

Modern childrearing practices place great emphasis on providing children with emotional literacy—that is, an ability to verbalize and express emotion. Never before has the importance of emotion been so fully recognized and appreciated. The reasons for this are various, but the underpinning philosophy, which has been scientifically documented, is that emotionally aware children who are capable of understanding and verbalizing their feelings are more successful and happy in all areas of their lives.

what kind of parent did you have?

Your parents are likely to have set the stage for the way you deal with emotions. Dismissive parents, who disregard, ignore, or trivialize emotions, are likely to create children

Emotionally aware people have been proven to be more self-motivated, more intuitive, better able to read other people's social cues (something called instinctive interaction), and better able to cope with the ups and downs of life. When you understand your emotions, can handle your feelings, and learn how to read and express hopes and fears, among other emotions, you will learn more about yourself, and how others respond to their emotions.

Understanding emotions provides the ability to regulate emotional states, and there is great comfort in the knowledge that emotions can be analyzed and dealt with, rather than suppressed or blurted out when least expected. When we discover our emotional literacy, we learn to empathize with ourselves, which is a cornerstone of self-understanding and self-love.

who suppress emotion, or feel a powerful distaste for or fear of emotions. They often see emotion in others as a sign of weakness, largely because they have been unable to accept and come to terms with their own emotional selves. Disapproving parents, who are critical of their children's displays of emotion and who may punish or reprimand emotional expression, are likely to produce children who are also fearful or ashamed of emotional expression.

But are relaxed parents any better? Parents who accept emotion and empathize with their children's emotional expression can help to create emotionally intelligent children, but only when they offer guidance and set limits that help children come to terms with their feelings. Children who are not provided with guidelines often feel out of control emotionally. Used to expressing their feelings, they may suffer from an inability to understand why they feel the way they do, and how they can channel these emotions to positive effect.

giving your emotions words

It's all too easy to dismiss the emotions we experience as being unnecessary or unwelcome. Yet, understanding them, working out their root cause, and considering how they can best be expressed is an important part of being able to communicate and, ultimately, being self-aware.

actually feeling. Take the time to analyze how you feel, and try to come up with words that actually describe what you are experiencing. For example, you may feel frustrated by a colleague's comments, or jealous of another worker's success. You may feel enraged by a failure to meet a

How many words form your emotional repertoire? Do you describe yourself regularly as being "angry," "sad," "stressed," "happy," or "upset," for example? Do you rely on the same set of words for a multitude of different feelings? Teaching yourself new words to describe your emotions helps to differentiate between them. It also makes them appear more controllable, and less frightening or embarrassing. For example, you may come home from a bad day at work, lose your cool, and snap at your family. You may define this as being "stressed," without looking at what caused the build-up of feelings, and what you are

deadline, or disappointed in yourself that you did not achieve a goal. You could feel annoyed by a long meeting that ate into time you had otherwise allocated, or envious that your partner had a much easier day. You could feel insecure, fearful, exhausted, self-doubting, or powerless, all of which manifest themselves as the same outward expression of emotion: anger.

All emotion is acceptable, but, defining it, breaking it down into parts, and giving it words helps to make the feeling containable. Emotions that once seemed mysterious and uncontrollable acquire boundaries and limits. They become more manageable and are not as frightening as they once were. When you work out, for example, why you feel angry, you realize that you can express the elements of that emotion individually. It's much easier to explain feelings of powerlessness than it is to "let rip," without really understanding why or what you are communicating.

Look for insights in the images and language your feelings evoke. If it's a negative image, see if you can turn it around into something more positive. For example, if you feel deeply depressed and saddened after a series of unsettling events, do you find your tears embarrassing? Do they leave

you ashamed? Or can you look at them in a different way. Tears can be cathartic, cleansing, and a huge relief from the pent-up emotion you are experiencing. Similarly, think of how you feel when you are angry. Do you "explode" or feel destructive? Anger can also provide a release, and it can be energizing to release feelings that would otherwise simmer away, causing untold damage beneath the surface.

Find different words for the feelings you regularly experience. Anger can be broken down into frustration, powerlessness, agitation, fury, hostility, or even simply passion. Thinking up new words helps you to understand exactly what it is you are feeling. Instead of your anger feeling out of control, and explosive, it becomes a manifestation of the different emotions you've experienced.

it's all too easy to dismiss emotions as being unnecessary or unwelcome

communicating emotions

Learning to communicate emotions is essential for health and well-being. When we suppress emotion, we create an imbalance in our overall health, opening the door to physical illness that can, in turn, create or exacerbate emotional problems.

Think of yourself when you were a newborn baby—a completely innocent, trusting, and fearless being who requires only love and acceptance. Somewhere along the line we learned that love is not always returned, and that it often has to be earned. We learn to doubt ourselves and our ability to achieve acceptance. When we are hurt we

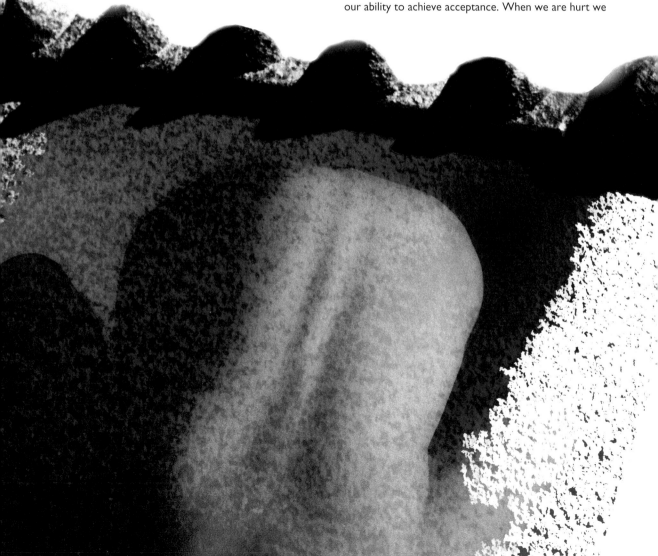

pretend that we do not want to be loved or to love. While this may sound simplistic, negative emotions almost always spring from an inability to trust or accept our feelings, and see the potential to make changes. In later life, suppressed feelings prevent us from opening up to others, which leads to fear, anxiety, insecurity, loneliness, and depression.

Although most emotional problems are rooted in upbringing, illness and stressful life events also take their toll. Depression is, for example, quite common after viral illnesses. Family, job, or financial pressures can also affect our ability to adapt. When considering your emotions, it's always worth reminding yourself that there can be other factors at work, and you need not blame yourself for feeling out of control, or believe that your feelings are out of control, when there may be an organic cause.

Many of us also find it difficult to express positive emotions—love, passion, joy, pure pleasure, and happiness. We can feel embarrassed by the depth of our feelings, guilty that others do not share our happiness, or suffer

from the "stiff upper lip" approach to communication, believing that emotions of any nature are best kept to oneself. It can, however, be just as damaging to suppress happy or positive emotions. Positive emotions—such as those we experience when we fall in love—can be life-enhancing, elating, and even overwhelming. Communicating these emotions helps us to feel more stable, more confident that what we are experiencing is normal and acceptable, and brings a sense of calm. We also learn more about ourselves when we see our own emotions reflected back through interaction with others.

It is not only for ourselves, however, that communicating emotion is important. To interact successfully with others, we need to adopt an emotional honesty that allows others to trust us, and feel they can express their own emotions without fear of reprisal.

There are several things to remember when considering how to express emotion. When we get to know ourselves, to understand, and to like ourselves, we will have the confidence to believe in what we think and feel. We should never need to defend, debate, or explain our thoughts, feelings, or actions. Before that, however, it is important to remember that what you do feel is valid. Recognize it, whether it is positive or negative, and ensure that you communicate that feeling. Never fall into the trap of feeling what you believe others think you should feel, or what you believe is expected of you.

It's important always to be the judge of your own thoughts, feelings, and actions. If you express yourself honestly, you are behaving with integrity. This type of integrity will feed self-confidence and engender the kind of trust and interaction that brings success in all areas of life. If you are judged negatively for what you have said or done, you can be certain that insecurity, jealousy, or negative emotions in others are at the root. Remain confident that what you have to say, what you feel, is acceptable. If you do not like or enjoy the way you are feeling, take the time to analyze it, and work out why. Never hesitate to follow your feelings. They are, ultimately, antennae—instinctive reactions to situations or people—that provide you with valuable insights that cannot always be explained on a conscious level. If you trust your own emotions, you will be able to use this instinct better, and to believe in it.

making your feelings known

Expressing ourselves, revealing something as private, or even base, as our innermost feelings and thoughts, can be daunting. Not many of us wish to present a window into our psyche to the outside world, and it's certainly inappropriate in many situations to do that. However, you will never achieve what you want, or impart to others the most basic elements of your personality and your vision, if you are not able to present yourself completely.

The first thing to remember is that there is always time. You never need to blurt out emotions, no matter how strongly you feel them. When you feel confident, you gain a

modicum of control that will allow you to express yourself in the most suitable way. When you feel a rush of emotion, stop and break it down, giving it words and descriptions. When confronting a colleague who has made you

extremely angry, for example, it is normally self-defeating to simply state that you are angry. A negative emotion has the tendency to create a negative energy that compounds the situation, and breeds mutual animosity. Try to express the components of your anger in a constructive way, offering solutions and showing respect for the emotions that your colleague might be experiencing himself. Begin by explaining that you are going to be honest, something that is always appreciated in any situation. Explain that you are feeling under pressure, perhaps insecure, or betrayed. When expressing emotion, it's important that you put it in the first person, never attributing blame or responsibility to others. After all, it is your emotion that you are sharing, whether or not it has been caused or created by interaction with others. Offer others a chance to respond in kind by saying, "How do you feel about that?" or "Do you agree with my perception of events?" Listen and respect their point of view, which is just as valid as your own. By sharing feelings, you are creating a communication channel that will be crucial to successful future interaction.

Try not to fear your emotions, whether they are positive or negative. You may feel hugely frightened by an expression of love for someone, for example, particularly if you are unsure of their feelings for you. Today, we are encouraged to play relationships "by the rules," which means pretending, acting, and suppressing natural emotions to ensure that the insecurities of others are maintained enough to guarantee their interest. This type of artificial interaction will never create or sustain an honest and loving relationship. You may feel vulnerable being honest, but you are expressing the person you really are, who you've grown to love and accept. If your emotions are not accepted, for whatever reason, it is worth considering the fact that your partner or friend is emotionally uncommitted, or even damaged in some way. Remind yourself that your emotions are valid, no matter what they are, and that expressing them honestly is a natural act.

The more you **understand** your own emotions,
the easier you will find it to **deal** with them when they arise

developing emotional awareness

Most of us would benefit from developing a deeper awareness of our emotional lives. You can use any of the meditations described in this book (see pages 34–39) or

express it creatively through music, perhaps, or writing. If you feel unable to express things orally, try writing words down on paper. This act will clarify your thoughts and help you to see the various components of the emotions you find yourself experiencing.

Building greater emotional awareness requires solitude, and it's important you take the time to get to know yourself better. Try also keeping an "emotion diary" (see chart opposite) as it can help you to observe whether a pattern exists. What makes you happy or sad? What makes you enraged or sulky? What causes great joy and elation? What makes you feel deep despair?

Writing things down can help you become more aware of incidents or thoughts that trigger your emotions, and how you react to them. When was the last time you cried or lost your temper? What led to this outburst of emotion? How did you feel about experiencing this emotion? Did you feel relieved afterward or ashamed? Were others aware that you were experiencing these feelings? Did you talk to anyone about the incident? You can also use the diary to make a note of your reactions to other people's emotions. What impact did they have on your own emotional state? Take some time at the end of each day to record your emotions, and work on becoming comfortable with them. The more you understand your own emotions, the easier you will find it to deal with them when they arise.

This type of diary can also be helpful for people who feel frightened or anxious about their emotional responses. The process of labeling an emotion and writing about it can help us to define and contain the feeling. Do you notice attitudes or preconceptions about emotion that you would like to change? Also, when we become sensitive to our own emotions, we are able to tune into other people's feelings.

emotion diary

the situation that resulted in heightened emotion

Who were you with?

What were you doing?

When was it?

Where were you?

initial automatic thoughts

What was going through my mind just before I started to feel this way?

What does this say about me?

What does this mean about me? My life? My future?

What am I afraid might happen?

What is the worst thing that could happen if this is true?

What does this mean about how the other person(s) feel(s)/think(s) about me?

What does this mean about the other person(s) or people in general?

What images or memories do I have of the situation?

moods   Describe each mood in one word. Rate intensity of mood (1-10).

evaluating your emotional health

Below are some questions that you can ask yourself to determine the current state of your emotional health.
To get an accurate result, answer the questions honestly.

1 *Can you tell others how you are feeling? This does not mean coming out with a simple, "I am sad," or "I am happy," response. It means being able to express your feelings at any time without being prodded.*

yes ☐   no ☐

2 *Do you exhibit signs of stress?*

yes ☐   no ☐

3 *Do you regularly feel listless or withdrawn?*

yes ☐   no ☐

4 *Do you laugh less than you used to?*

yes ☐   no ☐

5 *Do you smile or show delight easily?*

yes ☐   no ☐

6 *Do you become frustrated easily, and want to give up?*

yes ☐   no ☐

7 *Do you push yourself too hard to be the best— top of the sales team, best player on the pitch, the perfect parent, or the winner of the prize?*

yes ☐   no ☐

8 *Are you reluctant to take on new challenges that you would normally enjoy?*

yes ☐   no ☐

judging the results

If you answered yes to the first question, and no to all the others, you are very likely to be supremely balanced, and in touch with your emotions. Chances are, however, that you will have a mix of yes and no answers. Look at the areas where you answered yes. These indicate that there are parts of yourself and your life that are dissatisfying. If you boast, for example, you are likely to feel insecure and in need of attention. If you are attention-seeking, you probably do not feel confident enough to value yourself for who you are. If you are overly critical of others, you are likely to be displaying discontent with or dislike for parts of yourself.

This isn't a test, but rather, a way of examining areas of yourself that you may not be aware of, may not have acknowledged or accepted, or perhaps just do not like. Expressing the emotions that accompany each of these areas is one positive step toward self-awareness, self-acceptance, and positive interaction with others.

9 Do you get very upset if criticized or corrected?

yes ☐   no ☐

10 Do you put yourself down regularly?

yes ☐   no ☐

11 Are you overly critical of others?

yes ☐   no ☐

12 Do you try too hard to please people?

yes ☐   no ☐

13 Are you needy or insecure, or cling to the known?

yes ☐   no ☐

14 Do you suffer from inexplicable fears?

yes ☐   no ☐

15 Do you need continual approval?

yes ☐   no ☐

16 Do you boast?

yes ☐   no ☐

17 Are you aggressive or attention-seeking?

yes ☐   no ☐

18 Are you impatient and unappreciative?

yes ☐   no ☐

self-control

A measured response to any emotion is essential for successful communication. Too often, emotion that is expressed in the heat of the moment is discarded or trivialized. Putting your feelings across in a way that makes them understood, and allows you to feel that you have made yourself known, is an art that involves a certain amount of self-restraint and self-understanding. We all need to learn to manage our emotions so they are appropriate. We can do this by realizing what is behind a feeling, then finding ways to handle fears and anxieties, anger, sadness, and even joy. Begin by observing yourself, and recognizing a feeling as it happens. As you become accustomed to acknowledging your feelings you will more easily know what to expect—how it is normally diluted or eased, or how it can best be channeled to work in your favor. Channeling emotions toward a goal involves a certain amount of self-control and stifling of impulses. This does not mean stifling the emotion itself, however; it simply means using the energy of the emotion toward something positive. First and foremost, you must adopt a sensitivity to other people's feelings and concerns, and consider their perspective. Learn to appreciate the differences in how people feel about things.

analyze your emotions

Before you rush to express your emotions, consider what they are saying about you. For example, analyze your thoughts and feelings, and take steps to become more informed. If you feel critical, try to exercise

the art of patience

There will be times when it is simply impossible or ill-advised to express how you are feeling. However, the simple act of recognizing your emotion will help you to come to terms with it.

some compassion and work out why you feel the need to criticize others. If you feel insecure, use positive visualization or self-talk to create a deeper sense of security. When we label people, places, or situations, we rob ourselves of a growth opportunity. When we label our negative feelings, however, we identify our unmet emotional needs and the areas we need to work on in ourselves. Analyzing emotions in this way helps us to avoid falling into the trap of being too easily led by our emotions. While it is important to respond to the way we feel, to allow instinct to guide us, it also pays to have a healthy respect for the fact that we can be overwhelmed by feelings. When we lose control, we can act rashly—our judgment is clouded by emotion. Similarly, we can avoid seeing things through rose-tinted glasses (in the throes of positive emotion) or in a negative light if we take the time to analyze what we are feeling before we express our emotions and act.

Try a positive visualization exercise to channel the energy that your feeling has created. For example, if you are angry with someone, but expressing this anger is inappropriate (in the context of an office relationship, for example), consider the fact that you are tied to this person for as long as you hold this anger inside you. Imagine yourself literally tied, and imagine your anger being the bond. Visualize this

imagine yourself literally tied . . .

self-control   95

anger as a rope with many different sections. Give each
section a name, or let it represent one facet of your anger.
Imagine it being burned, or blown away, and then move on
to the next segment, until your tie is broken. Being tied to
others keeps you from growing emotionally. Research shows
that negative emotions (anger, depression, fear, guilt, jealousy)
have a negative effect on our body and mind. Dispersing these
negative emotions will make you feel more peaceful, more in
control of yourself, and happier. You are more likely to be a
greater success, and function better in the real world when
you are being guided by your positive emotions.

. . . and imagine
your anger being the bond

instinctive interaction

When we are in touch with our own emotions, and are comfortable sharing them, we acquire the ability to read the emotions of others. Empathy is the ability to identify with and understand another's situation, feelings, and motives. Observation skills help you to achieve this: You can learn to "read" what someone's emotional state is and you use this information to improve your ability to understand and to communicate.

Body language (see pages 146–151) offers a clue to emotions in others. Start by watching yourself. How do you hold your body—your arms, your head, your stance—when you are angry, absorbed, happy, upset, or insecure?

We show understanding, liking, and loyalty by aligning the upper body with others. During a meeting, for example, colleagues show support and agreement when they aim their torso in someone's direction (for example, the speaker's). Leaning forward suggests friendliness, while a "nonaligned" orientation indicates neutral or passive emotions that may graduate into dislike or disagreement. It's interesting to note that when women and men are in love, or have a great interest in or attraction to one another, they unthinkingly aim their upper bodies at partners, even if they angle their faces and eyes away.

According to the Center for Nonverbal Studies in the U.S., "We have a rich vocabulary of emotion cues expressing how we feel about ourselves and others. In the realm of emotion, words are often less trustworthy than nonverbal signs. This is because the latter cues are usually unintentional, involuntary, and unconscious." The eyes, nose, mouth, throat, and laryngeal openings are controlled by muscles and nerves from primitive tissues in our pharynx. Therefore, we may close (constrict) our facial features to show negative emotions (frowning or clearing our throats), and open (dilate) them to show pleasant feelings (raising an eyebrow, laughing, or smiling). When the sympathetic nervous system responds to fight-or-flight impulses (in the case of anxiety or embarrassment, for example), facial flushing becomes apparent.

When you become in tune with your own emotional cues, and the body language that accompanies them, you will instinctively see these patterns in others and be able to respond in an appropriate manner. You can also alter your own body language to send a message that either masks or reveals what you want to get across. For example, if you are

in a tricky situation and feel outrage or anger, you can control your body language (nodding for example, when the other person is talking, or turning your torso to face her). This type of communication helps to avoid confrontation, and sets the stage for a meaningful and positive interaction, allowing you to express your emotions in an unthreatening discourse.

As your sense of self-awareness develops and you become more in touch with your emotions and body language, you'll develop an intuition for how others are feeling. You'll also acquire the empathy to communicate successfully and honestly, giving others a true picture of what and who you are.

instant impressions

When we feel a rush of emotion—positive or negative—for a person or a situation, we learn something about ourselves. While it's important to go with our instincts to a certain extent, we must only do so when we have analyzed why we feel the way we do. Labeling our emotions is the first step (see pages 78–81), but we also must consider what they tell us about ourselves.

When we dislike characteristics in others, they tend to be features about ourselves that we dislike. For example, if we feel enraged by someone's tendency to butt in, or take over a discussion, chances are we tend to do the same thing ourselves—something we do not like about ourselves. Think carefully about why you have strong emotions for particular people. Look at their characters and try to find clues to characteristics you might share—or that you fear sharing. Before you judge others, and express negative emotions, ask yourself if your feelings are based on real factors, or if they are related to personal issues.

In many cases, our emotions reflect issues that began in childhood. For example, we may have been let down by a parent or a friend, and have an instinctive fear of betrayal. When we perceive that someone is betraying us now, we feel inordinate and disproportionate emotion. When the emotion is overwhelming and we blame others, it's important to realize that the root of the emotion we are experiencing can probably be found in our past.

Look back at your life and pinpoint situations when you experienced great or overwhelming emotion. Was that situation ever resolved? Have you carried a grudge, guilt, feelings of betrayal, or any other emotion into the present? Part of the process of learning to like yourself involves forgiving: Forgiving yourself for past transgressions, and

forgiving others for causing you pain. When past issues are resolved, you will know that the emotion you experience now is actually based on the current situation.

understanding anger

Very often, anger is a form of control. It is an attempt to force others to act the way we want them to act, to meet our needs in a situation by "doing things our way." We often justify our

anger by laying blame on others for perceived transgressions. Remember, however, that anger often hides deeper feelings, such as guilt, hurt, fear, or sadness, with which we have not come to terms. When we feel and show anger, we bring up parts of ourselves that need to be healed. Anger prevents us from taking steps to resolve a situation.

Our anger may be expressed as a direct attack, passive aggression, withdrawal, complaining, or suffering. All these forms are an attempt to gain control, rather than learn from the situation. Even if your anger succeeds in controlling, it still puts off a valuable lesson. Lack of confidence leads to controlling behavior and anger in its many forms.

what can your anger tell you about yourself?

Anger is almost always dispersed if we let ourselves understand and experience the deeper feelings beneath it, instead of attacking or withdrawing. If we get to know ourselves, we can come to terms with our more primordial emotions and resolve them. What can your anger tell you about yourself? What is it masking? Understanding ourselves is the key to understanding the nature of our emotions. Emotions provide valuable clues about who we are now, and what "baggage" we carry. By analyzing, understanding, and learning to express our emotions in a positive way, we hold in our hands one of the most powerful forms of communication, both with ourselves and with others.

When emotions are negative or suppressed, the creative urge is either quelled or distorted. If you choose to express your full creative potential, learning to effectively release trapped emotional stress is imperative. The joy that results in unimpeded creative expression or creative problem-solving is worth the effort expended to create emotional well-being in the body and mind. The body and mind are not separate from each other; they are extensions of one another, interconnected and interdependent. Emotions are the bridge that joins the energetic forces together, and the resulting pattern can be one of joy and appreciation for life. Clarity of mind, perfect health, and freedom of spirit is the pristine reward of emotional well-being.

your intelligent self

All of us share an intelligence and creativity that can be mined to produce the best possible lives for ourselves. It is only when we tap into this innate intelligence that we can get what we want from our lives.

The labels that we have acquired throughout our lives, and the limitations we impose upon ourselves, through either fear or lack of self-belief and confidence, create barriers to our own potential. Failure to use the potential of our minds leads to frustration, dissatisfaction, and a feeling that we are not living life to the fullest. Becoming our own best friend involves taking chances, acknowledging our true worth, and having the confidence to maximize our potential.

Beneath the surface, the real you has unlimited ability, unexplored depths, and untapped mental powers just waiting to be used. By learning to become more self-aware—exploring the parts of your mind that you may not even have known existed—you can acquire greater flexibility, enhanced intellect, creativity, and understanding, and the knowledge that you can do anything to which you set your mind.

WHAT LIES BENEATH

Despite years of research, science has come to few definitive conclusions about the brain, and vast areas remain a mystery.

the unused brain

It is difficult to assess accurately which parts of the brain are used for different processes, but postmortem examinations show there is different brain activity among people. When Einstein's brain was studied, for example, scientists discovered an unusually high number of glial cells in his parietal lobe. Glial cells support the neurons and the parietal lobe is thought to facilitate abstract thought. High counts of glial cells suggest that he was using this portion of his brain cognitively and extensively. We do know that whenever anything is learned, new dendrite connections are made between neurons. Greater usage of the brain through learning and stimulation creates greater "dendrite connectivity," and Einstein's brain indicated extensive dendrite connectivity.

Numerous studies show that if the brain is exercised beyond its current limits, new pathways are created. The scientific term for this is "use-dependent plasticity." This means that if a part of the brain isn't used, it will be lost. It also means that new parts of the brain can be accessed with use. One of the ways to use different parts of the brain is to avoid the trap of habitual thinking and, instead, reach beyond the obvious when considering problems and issues (see pages 110–115). With practice, new neural pathways can be opened in the mind and, if these pathways are activated regularly, they will become permanent.

it appears that we use only 10 percent of our brains

No brain research has ever shown a brain in which the entire neuron and synaptic connection potentials were used. In fact, it appears that we use roughly only ten percent of our brains, with possibly 90 percent scarcely touched. We do know that some people have been able to access other parts of their brain, often with what appears to be little effort. Take, for example, autistic people, many of whom have one unusual talent, such as the ability to perform incredibly difficult numerical tasks instantaneously or play a musical instrument without any training. These activities of clear genius indicate that the human brain is capable of greater achievements. There are also indications that the human brain is capable of miraculous activity, such as ESP (extra sensory perception). Or take the strict regime of some Tibetan monks, who can maintain body temperature and body weight while taking in no food and leaving themselves open to the elements for months at a time. In this case, they use their brains to maintain homeostasis and control over their autonomous nervous systems in a way that most of us could not begin to understand.

are you ready

to tap into your own

genius, your own

innate capacity to

work at a level

beyond

the average person?

Genius in any area—be it artistic, musical, mathematical, scientific, linguistic, or intellectual—provides clear evidence that certain individuals are using portions of their brain that the majority are not. No thought can be processed without the use of the brain. Therefore, if demonstrable feats of extraordinary mental, artistic, or psychic functioning exist in even a small group of people, it indicates that the human brain has capacities not tapped into by the majority.

The Einstein Factor, by Dr. Win Wenger and Richard Poe, details the essential mental qualities needed to create a genius, and how genius can unfold in anyone. Dr. Wenger notes, "…my studies have led me consistently to the conclusion that geniuses are little more than ordinary people who have stumbled upon some knack or technique for widening their channel of attention, thus making conscious their subtle, unconscious perceptions."

habitual thinking

Most of us use very little of our brains because we become accustomed to thinking and acting in predefined and habitual ways. We have all acquired behavioral programs through social, parental, genetic, and educational

Habitual thinking forms definite neural pathways of thought—ruts in the brain from which it can be difficult to extract ourselves. When we adopt flexible thinking, we create flexibility in our brains and in our minds.

conditioning. We follow the lead of others and behave in a similar way because this is what society seems to expect. The opposite, however, is not anarchy, but a sort of spontaneous creativity that defies conditioning. It opens the mind to solutions, to intuition, and to the vast fountain of knowledge and wisdom that lies within each of us.

Most education systems target logical, left-brain activity. Reading, writing, and math all use the structure of sequential thought. Even reasoning is attributed to left-brain thinking. By developing this part of the brain, our capacity for wisdom is limitless. The problem is, of course, that schooling structures the mind to use a series of predefined and tested methods to reach conclusions. Creativity and lateral thinking is stifled in a rote approach to education.

The right side of the brain is accessed and stimulated through art, sports, music, and other forms of sensory training. It can be stimulated by solving analogical puzzles and those that involve spatial orientation and the recognition of patterns. When we open neural pathways in the right side of the brain, we develop insight—we suddenly know the solution to problems. Insight is a prerequisite for genius. We realize the answer is in our brains, and with practice, we can access it. To develop self-awareness, we need to unravel our thought habits and understand that our conditioned "ego" response masks spontaneous self-awareness and intuition. To do this, allow yourself to think as a child does, without the clutter of conditioned responses to everything. Allow yourself to become detached from what you consider to be reality, and let your mind flow in whatever direction it takes. According to J. L. Reid, creator of the web site, Enchanted Mind: The Science Behind Creative Thinking (*www.enchantedmind.com*), "Truly creative people can stop at any moment, view what they are doing, and see a sincerely original and resolute answer to whatever question they ask. This is because they don't live for other people's opinions, nor do they have to look outside themselves for answers to difficult questions. They know instinctively that within themselves, hidden within the creative mind, the answer lies waiting to be discovered.

"The creative mind is always present in that gap between a conditioned ego response and a spontaneous self-aware intuitive moment. It can be learned. It has always been within you, it just grows dimmer as we get used to not allowing it as we did when we were children. Dive into the gap head first, allow your heart to follow. When you emerge, your whole psyche will be cleansed and clarified, and a bit of spontaneous joy will leave its mark on your mind. Inner creativity is only a moment away."

eight patterns of limited thinking

In the book *Thoughts and Feelings: Taking Control of Your Moods and Life*, Dr.s McKay, Davis, and Fanning discuss a method of challenging automatic thoughts in order to counter perfectionism, curb procrastination, and open the mind to intuition. The patterns of limited thinking and their resolution (or balancing thought) are shown below.

Breaking these patterns of limited, habitual thought and the automatic methods you use to approach matters will help you to expand your mind to accept other possibilities. What's more, you'll become a more compassionate person, able to forgive others for their differences and any shortcomings, as you are able to forgive yourself.

1

overgeneralization

In this pattern, you make a broad, general conclusion based on a single incident or piece of evidence. One dropped stitch leads you to conclude, "I'll never learn how to knit." This can lead to an increasingly restricted life. For example, if you got sick on a train once, you decide never to take a train again. Overgeneralizations are often couched in the form of absolute statements using words such as all, every, none, never, always, everybody, and nobody. For example, you are overgeneralizing when you emphatically conclude, "Nobody loves me," or "I'll never be able to trust anyone again."

Another hallmark is the global label for persons, places, and things you don't like. Somebody who refused to give you a ride home, for instance, is labeled a "total jerk." Television is considered an "evil, corrupting influence." You're told you're "stupid" and "wasting your life." Each of these labels may contain a grain of truth, but it generalizes that grain into a global judgment. The overgeneralized label ignores all contrary evidence, making your view of the world stereotyped and one-dimensional.

quantify

Ask yourself for evidence and tell yourself there are no absolutes. If your conclusion is based on one or two cases, a single mistake, or one small symptom, then throw it out until you have more convincing proof.

Fight overgeneralization by quantifying. For example, if you catch yourself thinking, "We're buried under massive debt," rephrase the statement with a quantity, "We owe $27,000."

Stop thinking in absolutes by replacing words such as every, all, always, none, never, everybody, and nobody with words such as may, sometimes, and often. These words allow for exceptions and shades of gray. Be particularly sensitive to future predictions, such as "No-one will ever love me." They are extremely dangerous because they can become self-fulfilling prophecies.

Replace negative terms with more neutral ones. If you call your habitual caution cowardice, replace it with care. Instead of lazy, call yourself laid-back.

2

polarized thinking

This is black-and-white thinking, with no shades of gray. You make "either/or" choices, perceiving everything at one extreme with very little room for middle ground. People and things are good or bad, wonderful or horrible, delightful or intolerable. Since your interpretations are extreme, your emotional reactions are also extreme, fluctuating from despair, rage, or terror to elation and ecstasy.

The greatest danger in polarized thinking is its impact on how you judge yourself. You believe that if you aren't perfect or brilliant, then you must be a failure or an imbecile. There's no room for mistakes or mediocrity.

avoid black-or-white judgments

People are not either happy or sad, loving or rejecting, brave or cowardly, smart or stupid. Humans are just too complex to be reduced to "either/or" judgments. If you have to make these kinds of ratings, think in terms of percentages. For example, "About 30 percent of me is scared to death, and 70 percent is coping," "About 60 percent of the time he seems terribly preoccupied with himself, but there's the 40 percent when he can be really generous," or "Five percent of the time I'm an idiot, the rest of the time I do all right."

3

filtering

This is characterized by a sort of tunnel vision—looking at only one element of a situation to the exclusion of everything else. A single detail is picked out and the whole event or situation is colored by this detail. For example, you may have achieved a goal and been praised by all of your colleagues. One, however, noted that it took you a long time. You will filter out the praise and focus only on the criticism, even though this was only a small part of the experience.

Memory can also be very selective. You may remember only certain kinds of events from your entire history and stock of experiences. When you filter your memories, you often pass over positive experiences and dwell only on the memories that characteristically leave you angry, anxious, depressed, insecure, and doubtful.

shift focus

To conquer filtering, deliberately shift your focus. This can be done in two ways. First, place your attention on strategies for dealing with the problem rather than obsessing about the problem itself. Second, focus on the opposite of your primary mental theme. For example, if you tend to focus on the theme of loss, focus instead on what you still have that is of value. If your theme is danger, focus on the things in your environment that represent comfort and safety instead. If your theme is injustice, stupidity, or incompetence, shift your focus to the things others do that meet with your approval. New patterns of thinking help us to escape the ruts to which we limit ourselves.

mind reading

When you mind read, you make snap judgments about others. You assume you know how others are feeling and what motivates them: "He's just acting that way because he's jealous," "She's only interested in your money," 'He's afraid to show he cares."

As a mind reader, you also make assumptions about how people are reacting to you. You might assume what your boyfriend is thinking and say to yourself, "He sees how unattractive I am without makeup." If he is mind reading too, he may be saying to himself, "She thinks I'm really immature." You may have a casual encounter with your supervisor at work and come away thinking, "They're getting ready to fire me." These assumptions are born of intuition, hunches, vague misgivings, or a couple of past experiences. They are unprovable, but you believe them nonetheless.

Mind reading depends on a process called projection. You imagine that people feel the same way you do and react to things the same way you do. Therefore you don't watch or listen closely enough to notice that they are actually different. If you become angry when someone is late, you imagine everyone feels that way. If you feel excruciatingly sensitive to rejection, you expect that most people are the same. If you are very judgmental about particular habits and traits, you assume others share your beliefs.

ask yourself for evidence

In the long run, you are probably better off making no inferences about people at all. Either believe what they tell you or hold no belief at all until some conclusive evidence comes your way. Treat all of your notions about people as hypotheses to be tested and checked out by asking them.

Sometimes you can't check out your interpretations. For instance, you may not be ready to ask your daughter if her withdrawal from family life means she's pregnant or taking drugs. But you can allay your anxiety by generating alternative interpretations of her behavior. Perhaps she's in love. Or premenstrual. Or studying hard. Or depressed about something. Or deeply engrossed in a project. Or worrying about her future. By generating a string of possibilities, you may find a more neutral interpretation that's as likely to be true as your worst suspicions. This process also underlines the fact that you really can't accurately know what others are thinking and feeling unless they tell you.

By all means, use your intuition and allow it to guide you, but beware of making assumptions that may reflect yourself rather than the reality of someone else.

catastrophizing

If you "catastrophize," a small leak in the sailboat means it will surely sink. A contractor whose estimate gets underbid concludes he'll never get another job. A headache suggests that brain cancer is looming. Catastrophic thoughts often start with the words "What if?" You read a newspaper article describing a tragedy or hear gossip about some disaster befalling an acquaintance, and you start wondering, "What if it happens to me? What if I break my leg skiing? What if they hijack my plane? What if I get sick and have to go on disability? What if my son starts taking drugs?" The list is endless. There are no limits to a really fertile, catastrophic imagination.

explore the odds

Catastrophizing is the royal road to anxiety. As soon as you catch yourself catastrophizing, ask yourself, "What are the odds?" Make an honest assessment of the situation in terms of odds or percent of probability. Are the chances of disaster one in 100,000 (0.001 percent)? One in a thousand (0.1 percent)? One in twenty (5 percent)? Looking at the odds helps you realistically evaluate whatever it is that is frightening you.

magnifying

When you magnify, you emphasize things out of proportion to their actual importance. Small mistakes become tragic failures. Minor suggestions become scathing criticism. A slight backache becomes a ruptured disk. Minor setbacks become cause for despair. Slight obstacles become overwhelming barriers. The flip side of magnifying is minimizing. When you magnify, you view everything negative and difficult in your life through a telescope that enlarges your problems. But when you view your assets, such as your ability to cope, you look through the wrong end of the telescope so that everything positive is minimized.

get things in proportion

To combat magnifying, stop using words like terrible, awful, disgusting, and horrendous. In particular, banish phrases such as, "I can't stand it," "It's impossible," or "It's unbearable." You can stand it, because history shows that human beings can survive almost any psychological blow and can endure incredible physical pain. You can get used to and cope with almost anything. Try saying to yourself phrases such as "I can cope" and "I can survive this."

personalization

There are two kinds of personalization. The first involves directly comparing yourself with other people, "He plays piano so much better than I do," "I'm the slowest person in the office." Sometimes the comparison is actually favorable to you: "I am more clever than he is" or "I am better looking." The opportunities for comparison never end. And, even when the comparison is favorable, the underlying assumption is that your worth is questionable. Consequently, you must continue to test your value, constantly measuring yourself against others. If you come out better, you have a moment's relief. If you come up short, you feel diminished.

Personalization also involves the tendency to relate everything to yourself. A depressed mother blames herself when she sees any sadness in her children. A businessman thinks that every time his partner complains of being tired, he really means he's tired of him. A man whose wife complains of rising prices hears an attack on his ability as a breadwinner.

stop comparing

We all have strong and weak points, and comparison is meaningless. When you catch yourself making comparisons, remind yourself that everyone has strong and weak points. By matching your weak points to other people's strong points, you are just looking for ways to demoralize yourself. If you assume that the reactions of others are often about you, force yourself to check it out. Maybe the reason the boss is frowning isn't that you're late. Draw no conclusion unless you're satisfied that you have reasonable evidence and proof.

8

shoulds

In this pattern, you operate from a list of inflexible rules about how you and other people should act. The rules are right and indisputable. Any deviation from your particular values or standards is bad. As a result, you are often judging others and finding fault. People irritate you. They don't act correctly and they don't think correctly. They have unacceptable traits, habits, and opinions that make them hard to tolerate. They should know the rules, and they should follow them.

Your shoulds are just as hard on you as they are on other people. You feel compelled to be or act a certain way, but you never ask objectively if it really makes sense. The German-American psychiatrist Karen Horney called this "the tyranny of shoulds."

Some of the most common and unreasonable shoulds include, "I should be the epitome of generosity, consideration, dignity, courage, and unselfishness," "I should be the perfect lover, friend, parent, teacher, student, or spouse," "I should be able to endure any hardship with equanimity," "I should be able to find a quick solution to every problem," "I should never feel hurt; I should always be happy and serene," "I should know, understand, and foresee everything," "I should always be spontaneous, but also always control my feelings," "I should never feel certain emotions, such as anger or jealousy," "I should love my children equally," "I should never make mistakes," "My emotions should be constant," "Once I feel love, I should always feel love," "I should be totally self-reliant," "I should assert myself, but I should never hurt anybody else," and "I should never be tired or get sick."

accept individuality and be flexible

Re-examine any personal rules or expectations that include the words should, ought, or must. Flexible rules and expectations don't use these words because there are always exceptions and special circumstances. Think of at least three exceptions to your rule.

You may become irritated when people don't act according to your values. But your personal values are just that, personal. They may work for you, but, as missionaries have discovered all over the world, they don't always work for others. People aren't all the same. The key is to focus on each person's uniqueness—his or her particular needs, limitations, fears, and pleasures. Because it is impossible to know all of these complex interrelations, even with your nearest and dearest, you can't be certain whether your values apply to another. You are entitled to an opinion, but allow for the possibility of being wrong. Also, allow for other people to find different things important.

thought awareness

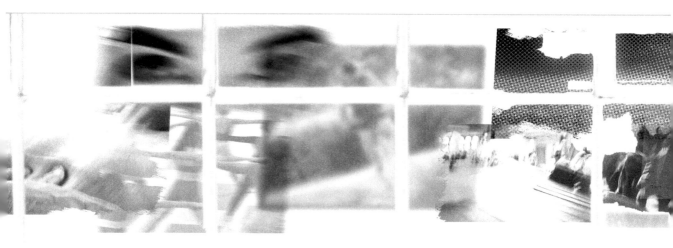

This is the process by which you observe your thoughts for a time, perhaps when you are under stress, to become aware of what is going through your head. It allows you to witness where your thinking has become stagnant or habitual, and provides valuable insight into yourself, letting you see where you can suspend thought and allow your subconscious to direct your thinking.

Find a quiet room and prepare yourself for meditation (see page 34). Watch your thoughts go by. Try not to suppress any thoughts, whether they are negative or positive—just let them run their course while you observe. You may not even notice that your thoughts exist until you begin to observe your stream of consciousness. The reason for this is a type of "self-preservation" thinking. In other words, feelings of inadequacy, self-criticism, or dwelling on the consequences of a poor performance may flit into your consciousness, but be instantly suppressed or ignored because they pose a threat to your equilibrium.

Pay particular attention to negative thoughts. Make a note of them and continue to watch them. This is the first step to eliminating negative self-beliefs—you cannot counter thoughts you did not realize you were thinking.

tapping into the subconscious

There is no doubt that the subconscious exists. It is a type of instinctive or intuitive brain activity that guides and directs the body, keeping our hearts working, our lungs breathing, and our instincts sharp. There is also evidence

that the subconscious is the home of the psyche. The subconscious can be raised to conscious awareness, and the full potential of the psyche unveiled.

The problem is that many of us have thoughts that clutter our consciousness, that prevent us from delving deeper to that place of creative, intuitive thinking. Once you have mastered thought awareness, you will be able to delve beneath your thoughts (which can continue to run in background, rather like unchallenging music) and free up your creativity and thinking.

Many of us have experienced an "epiphany"—a moment of insight when something becomes crystal clear. We feel we know the answer to something that has been troubling us; we feel as if a burst of light has surfaced. Intuitive thought is a sudden, complete understanding that comes forward from the subconscious, in an unexpected way. The creative psyche is opened, and wisdom is released.

This deeper mind is available to us whenever we call on it. Many branches of psychology are now focusing on the different ways we can access this portion of consciousness that lies below the surface. The interesting thing is that we the minutiae of daily life and thinking to be quieted, and allowing the subconscious (which can be considered the place of all innate knowledge) to break through. This can be experienced as a very dramatic moment—a bit like a

are constantly bombarded with intuition and insight from our subconscious—answers and solutions that are normally not even noted, or dismissed because they do not fall into the realms of rational thought or action. One of the products of habitual thinking is that we become so deeply imbedded in the accepted way of acting, responding, and drawing conclusions that we simply do not register the messages of wisdom from our subconscious.

This highly unused portion of our mind can see the entire picture of any given situation. It knows the answer. It knows that the answer was in the question. Pure analogical thought doesn't rely on time or space, so it whispers the answer to our conscious mind almost instantly. The problem is, most of us are so entrenched in our usual linear modes of thinking, we ignore this whisper. Meditation can change the way you see things by letting

light going on in your mind. Every one of these moments of enlightenment serves to produce an easier path to the subconscious, and the awakening of unfrequented, often wonderful, pathways in our brains.

Remember that "energy follows thought." Your thoughts predispose you to view everything in a particular way. Habitual thinking creates very strong patterns that can be hard to break. What kind of thoughts fill your mind? Watch your thoughts through meditation and discover the patterns they most often fall into. Even long-standing patterns can be changed through awareness. Being trapped in habitual patterns of negative thinking can make you less productive and less efficient. Take time to break the patterns and allow your creative self to emerge.

Learn to view information through insight rather than through your habitual thinking patterns. Try to develop both intellect and intuition. You will, throughout your life, encounter many new ideas, many of which will be thrown up by your subconscious. Learn to trust these, and be open to other ways of looking at the world.

self-awareness

Much of this book focuses on self-awareness, which is the key to becoming the person you most greatly admire and love. Many religious and philosophical disciplines—including Zen, Taoism, and Buddhism—depend on the practice of self-awareness. They use meditation, or simply constant self-monitoring, to achieve a detached frame of mind in order to watch daily actions in a nonjudgmental way.

When learned and applied, this technique can be used as a tool to bridge the gap between the ego and the unconscious, allowing greater clarity of mind to unfold.

Remember that the mind is infinite. Its only boundaries are those you have created yourself. Find those boundaries and deliberately pass them, opening yourself to the unlimited possibilities of your mind.

Increase your self-knowledge by observing your emotions. Observe your different states of mind as they arise. Actions often occur without any conscious thought; patterns of behavior are repeated, leaving no opportunity for change. Self-awareness gives you a different view. You can see the patterns and change them yourself, choosing how to behave or react at any given point. A moment of personal insight can be gained by practicing mindfulness, bringing with it a whole new way of looking at the world.

And when we can see the humor in things, we can see the moments that usually go unnoticed when we act from habitual behavioral patterns. Humor embellishes the absurd, and celebrates the unusual or quirky, all of which open the mind to originality and inventive thought.

MAINTAIN SOFT FOCUS

Being aware of everything without focusing on one thing increases your peripheral vision. When you create and maintain soft-focus, the ego is temporarily set aside and the subconscious mind comes to the surface.

puzzles to enhance the mind

Zen is an ancient system of thought where enlightenment is brought about by introspection and insight. It differs from other faiths and philosophies in that it does not rely on habitual forms of thought or thinking to answer the questions that life presents to us. One of the central points of Zen is intuitive understanding. As a result, words and sentences have no fixed meaning, and logic is often irrelevant. Words have meaning only in relation to who is using them, to whom they are being spoken, and in what situation they are used.

Zen monks are given a koan to contemplate. Koans are apparently impossible puzzles—problems without solutions—and their purpose is to push a trainee beyond the bounds of linear thinking. Linear thinking involves using habitual thought patterns toward solutions. In other words, looking for obvious answers in obvious places. There is no answer to a koan, at least in our logical frame of mind. But, in Zen, there is no such thing as an impossible question or problem. The answer is to be found in the question and within ourselves. We need only to access it by suspending the way we normally think, and by allowing our intuition to provide us with an answer instead. Consider the parable of the single clapping hand opposite.

the sound of one hand clapping

The master of Kennin temple was called Mokurai or Silent Thunder. He had a protégé named Toyo who was only 12 years old. Toyo saw the older disciples visit the master's room each morning and evening to receive instruction in sanzen, or personal guidance, during which they were given koans to stop their minds from wandering.

Toyo wished to do sanzen also.

"Wait a while," said Mokurai. "You are too young."

But the child insisted, so the teacher finally consented. In the evening, little Toyo went at the proper time to the threshold of Mokurai's sanzen room. He struck the gong to announce his presence, bowed respectfully three times outside the door, and went to sit before the master in respectful silence.

"You can hear the sound of two hands when they clap together," said Mokurai. "Now show me the sound of one hand clapping."

Toyo bowed and went to his room to consider this problem. From his window he could hear the music of the geishas. "Ah, I have it!" he proclaimed. The next evening, when his teacher asked him to illustrate the sound of one hand, Toyo began to play the music of the geishas.

"No, no," said Mokurai. "That will never do. That is not the sound of one hand. You've not got it at all."

Thinking that such music might interrupt, Toyo moved his abode to a quiet place. He meditated again. "What can the sound of one hand be?" Toyo thought. He happened to hear some water dripping. "I have it," thought Toyo. When he next appeared before his teacher, Toyo imitated dripping water.

"What is that?" asked Mokurai. "That is the sound of dripping water, but not the sound of one hand. Try again."

In vain, Toyo meditated to hear the sound of one hand clapping. He heard the sighing of the wind. But the sound was rejected by Mokurai. He heard the cry of an owl. This also was refused. The sound of one hand was not the locusts.

Toyo visited Mokurai more than ten times with different sounds. All were wrong. For almost a year he pondered what the sound of one hand clapping might be. At last little Toyo entered true meditation and transcended all sounds.

"He could collect no more," Mokurai explained later, "so he reached the soundless sound."

Toyo had realized the sound of one hand clapping.

Puzzles use both sides of the brain to open our minds and push the boundaries of habitual thought, opening new pathways in the brain. By undertaking to move beyond your normal thought processes, and look for answers in your own subconscious, you will be taking a step toward releasing your innate creativity.

The web site *www.enchantedmind.com* offers daily puzzles for both the left and right side of the brain. It claims that "most of the time the answer will be intuited, perhaps after some contemplation. Contemplation is different from 'figuring out.' When you contemplate something, you ponder it from all sides. If you're skilled at this, you become the problem that you're working on. Once you become it, the solution will reveal itself almost as if by magic. As you do this more often, the simple, elegant solution becomes immediately apparent to you."

Attempt the two types of puzzle found on the opposite page. How well did you fare? Try to do the puzzles on the Enchanted Mind web site daily and you'll see your potential for creativity, enlightenment, and wisdom expand.

left brain puzzle

right brain puzzle

throw it overboard

A boat floating on a lake has some heavy pieces of iron in its hold. If the iron is thrown overboard, does the level of the lake rise, stay the same, or fall?

the coffee drinker

A man in a restaurant complains to the waiter that there is a fly in his cup of coffee. The waiter takes the cup away and promises to bring a fresh cup of coffee. He returns a few moments later. The man tastes the coffee and complains that this was his original cup of coffee with the fly removed. He is correct, but how did he know this?

solutions

The initial displacement of the boat is a volume of water whose weight is that of the boat (including the iron). By throwing the iron overboard, the displacement of the boat is decreased by a volume of water whose weight is that of the iron. The iron at the bottom of the lake will occupy a smaller volume and hence the level of the lake will fall.

The man had sweetened his first cup of coffee with sugar.

image streaming

This technique was pioneered by Dr. Wenger, coauthor of *The Einstein Factor*, who believes that awareness of subtle unconscious perceptions is the key to genius. In essence, image streaming is an exercise where you describe an observation aloud to a tape recorder or another person, then examine your perceptions as you speak. The process is said to draw larger portions of unconscious thought into your consciousness. This is due to the belief that we are all born thinking in images, that is, we have a database of images that represents an awareness in our subconsciousness. This awareness allows us to find understanding and anwers to questions.

According to Dr. Wenger, "It's important to describe aloud, to bring the mind's images into conscious awareness, no matter how unrelated the images may at first appear. This process helps bridge the separate regions of the brain. Let yourself be surprised by what your images reveal—the more surprising, the more likely that you're getting fresh input from your subtler, more comprehensive faculties."

To start image streaming, Dr. Wenger says, "Pick out a feature from your imagination—a wall, a tree, or bush—whatever's there. Imagine laying a hand on that feature and studying how it feels. Describe that feeling to strengthen your contact with the experience. Ask that rock or bush or wall, 'Why are you here?' See if the imagery changes when you ask that question, then describe any changes. Once you've run through a set of images, thank your image streaming faculties for showing you this answer. Ask for their help in understanding the messages in your images, as they are often symbolic.

"Repeat the process by starting a new image stream with entirely different images that nonetheless somehow still give you the same answer to the same question. After two to three minutes of this new imagery, repeat the process to get a third set of images, each different, yet each showing the same answer in a different way.

"Examine whatever's the same among the several sets of images when all else is different. These themes or elements-in-common are your core answer or message. Now go back to your original question, 'Why are you here?' and determine in what ways these core elements are the answer.

"Summarize the whole experience to another person or into a notebook or computer. This change of medium, and change of feedback, should add further to your understanding."

putting on the heads

This is an ancient technique of assuming the identity of someone you wish to emulate. By pretending to be that person, and performing whatever talent that person has, you give your own subconscious a clear experience of that talent. If you practice daily, your subconscious will indeed take on that talent and you'll begin to express it.

Athletic trainers have been using this technique for years to improve performance. Indeed, there is some evidence that practicing a talent in your mind is equivalent to, if not more powerful than, actual physical practice. In your mind you can practice something perfectly and create a neural network of perfect execution. This is one of the most powerful techniques you can use to become anything you desire.

brainstorming

A lateral thinking process, brainstorming is an excellent way of developing creative solutions to a problem. It opens your mind to intuition and thoughts beyond the normal circuitous patterns. It works by focusing on a problem, then coming up with many very radical solutions. Ideas should be as broad and deliberately odd as possible, and they should be developed as fast as possible. Brainstorming is designed to help you break out of your old thinking patterns and find new ways of looking at things. During brainstorming sessions there should be no criticism of ideas—you are trying to open possibilities and break down wrong assumptions about the limits of the problem. Judgment and analysis at this stage will stunt idea generation. Ideas should only be evaluated once the brainstorming session has finished, when you can further explore solutions using more conventional approaches.

When you brainstorm on your own you will produce a wider range of ideas than you would in a group session, since you do not have to worry about other people's egos or opinions, and can therefore be more free in your creativity. However, you may not develop as many effective ideas since you do not have a group to help you.

Group brainstorming, on the other hand, can be very effective because it uses the experience and creativity of all members of the group. When individual members reach their limit on an idea, another member's creativity and experience can take the idea to the next stage. Group brainstorming therefore tends to develop ideas in more depth than individual brainstorming.

what to do

Clearly define the problem you want to solve, and make sure you lay out any criteria that need to be met. Keep your thoughts clearly focused on the problem. Have fun!

Try to come up with as many ideas as possible, from solid practical ones to wildly impractical ideas. Spark your own creativity. Avoid following any train of thought for too long. If you become stuck for ideas, choose a word from the dictionary (a noun is most useful), and find a way of working it into the solution. You may find yourself coming up with far-fetched ideas and considerations, but these are equally valid because you are allowing your mind to wander outside its normal confines.

Always keep a note of the ideas that come out of your brainstorming session, and after the session study and evaluate them. In their midst will be the solution.

lucid dreaming

This term describes the experience of recognizing during a dream that you are dreaming. By involving your conscious awareness in a subconscious activity, you can learn to control the content of your dream and its course of action.

You will also remember these dreams more easily. Lucid dreams are often more vivid than simple visualizations. Objects and people appear to be and feel solid, and the dreamer is often able to converse intelligently with his own dream characters. Lucid dreamers can create or eliminate characters and objects in their dream, and can also access their short- and long-term memories.

One technique for achieving a lucid dream state is to ask yourself the question, "Is this a dream?" or "Am I dreaming?" about 25 times just before falling asleep. The conscious repetitiveness of the question will eventually be submerged into the subconscious dream state. Reflecting cognitively upon the question in the dream state may result in some form of conscious intervention and awareness, and a lucid dream state can result.

You can also use a stimulus response link. For instance, just before going to sleep, look at your hand while reiterating to yourself over and over, "When I see my hand in my dream, I will know I am dreaming."

These techniques will produce an ability to achieve lucid dreaming in four to five weeks or less. After achieving a lucid dream state, act only as a casual observer at first, otherwise, the condition might quickly dissipate into wakefulness.

Why lucid dreaming? The dream experience is perhaps the most creative form of consciousness that some people will ever experience. If you recall your dreams upon waking, you can take the symbols, images, and adventures you experienced and discover what is going on at deeper levels of your psyche. This is incredibly valuable information that will improve creative potential and open your mind to parts of yourself that are only experienced during sleep.

DREAMING TO DISSOLVE FEARS

As you slowly integrate volitional control and alterations into your dreams, you will achieve full dream mastery. Using lucid dreaming in this way can help you overcome any phobias and fears, such as flying.

doodling and reading symbols

One way to access the higher or underpinning parts of your mind is through doodling. While this may sound impossibly simple, many symbols are thrown up from your subconscious, and can prove to be answers to problems or insights into yourself.

Symbols can be read on two levels. You can analyze them through a book that attributes universal meaning (see box opposite) or you can intuitively understand their meanings by looking at their relevance to your own life and asking yourself (perhaps while meditating, or at least clearing your mind of mental clutter) what they mean to you. Doodling allows our intuitive feelings to express themselves in pictorial, symbolic form. Interpreting these symbols can help to unveil meanings that are not apparent to our linear mind. A symbol conveys an entire thought in one image. Language depends upon a linear procession of symbols to convey a thought. Doodling allows the unconscious to come to the surface without judgment or critical analysis from the conscious mind.

how to doodle

Focus on something that you are attempting to create or resolve. Hold the initial idea or desire in the mind and allow yourself to go into a blank stare or soft focus, preferably on a neutral background (the sky, a white wall, neutral carpet). As ideas and feelings come to the mind, simply doodle them onto a piece of clean white paper.

When you have finished doodling, set the paper aside for a period of time. When your mind is fresh look at what you've drawn. You will begin to get feelings or ideas. You may even see actual structures in the doodles. You may have unconsciously drawn the solution to your problem.

Look at the symbols and choose how you wish to interpret them. Clear your mind and look at what you have produced. If you do not see anything meaningful, leave it for a period of time and come back to it. You may have included words or numbers. How are these relevant to

you? If nothing springs to mind, consider brainstorming (see page 128–129). Again, jot down anything that immediately comes to mind. The answer will be there on your paper—a message from your unconscious. The potential and capacity of our minds is limitless. It may take time to master the techniques necessary to unharness the creativity and intelligence that lies within you, but with time and practice, you will become adept at using intuitive thought to bring forth wisdom and enlightenment from the farthest reaches of your mind. The key is to change the way you think, to embrace the unlikely, the untried, the new, and the different. Be open to insight—watch your own thoughts, and allow them to spin and turn until they throw up information and ideas beyond the normal scope of habitual thinking. As you become more self-aware, you will find parts of yourself that you did not know existed, parts of your brain that move you toward the kind of self-knowledge, success, and self-love that we all desire.

interpreting dreams and symbols

Bridges may symbolize transition. Freud gives the example of a woman who wants to be a man, and consequently dreams of bridges that don't quite reach the other side of the river. However, the symbolized change may be something that can be achieved more easily, but still possibly requiring will and determination. For example, a change of lifestyle or passing from middle years into old age.

Water is a common symbol for fertility, growth, creative potential (especially if it takes the form of a reservoir or still lake), new life, or healing. It also symbolizes the unconscious, especially if it is deep. An ocean or the sea is a good representation of the deep unconscious.

The sun may be a symbol of your true and total self, or of the conscious ego. It may symbolize intelligence, as distinct from intuition, and may also represent a father or authority figure, someone who is silently judging you.

The moon has always been regarded as the source of fertility, governing, as it does, ocean tides and rainfall, menstruation and birth. According to Australian Aboriginal tradition, the moon makes women pregnant. It is also the symbol of personal growth.

Fish are also common symbols of fertility which, in psychological terms, means (a promise of) personal growth. If the fish are in the sea, the sea may symbolize the unconscious, the fish unconscious urges (such as over-eating). According to the psychoanalyst Carl Jung, fish, being cold-blooded and primitive creatures, may also symbolize a deep level of unconsciousness. They can also represent libido or greed.

how to communicate

The act of communicating with others is crucial to our happiness. If we are unable to express ourselves, relate to people, and interact with confidence and honesty, we not only become frustrated and stagnant, but we also rob ourselves of one of the richest parts of being human.

Communication is, ultimately, an exchange of energies and ideas that opens the mind to greater possibilities. When we connect with others, we encourage the kind of energy flow, discourse, and communication that feeds our self-image and helps us to understand ourselves.

No one can achieve success without being able to communicate their ideas, vision, purpose, and personalities clearly and calmly to the world around them. Good communication ensures that needs are met and identities preserved in the face of external criticism or skepticism.

Communication facilitates rewarding and lasting relationships, and from good relationships springs the confidence necessary to develop self-awareness, to believe in ourselves, and to achieve our dreams.

the role of energy

All human interchange involves energy flow. Some people have a compatible energy (called an animating force) that draws us in. Others have the ability to drain us—the product of an incompatible or discordant energy. When we interact with others, we need to be aware of the role of energy. Consider the role of instinct when you first meet someone. You may feel an immediate bond or natural affinity. On the other hand, you may experience instant and intangible dislike. The force at work here is energy. We may already be sensitive to the energy of others or aware of the impact our own energy has. As parents, we see the impact negative energy has on our children: A baby becomes anxious and cries when his mother is distressed, a child throws a temper tantrum when his father is rushed and under pressure. Many mothers claim that their children are the most badly behaved when they themselves do not feel they have the resources to cope—at the end of an exhausting day, before menstruation, while preparing a meal, or organizing the house for guests. The reason for this is that parents transmit energy, negative and positive. When you are feeling calm, your children respond by acting calmly. If you are wound up, they will be too.

When we give out negative energy, we get it back. When we offer love and positive energy, it is passed on.

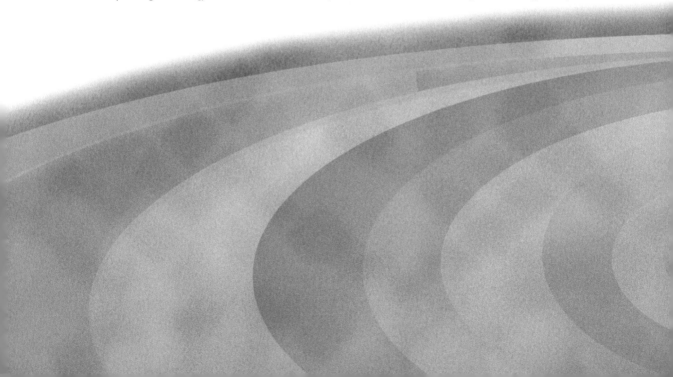

Watch the effect of a positive encounter, the way it has a rippling effect outward. Smile at someone for no reason and they will smile back. Radiate peace, confidence, and self-love, and others will absorb it and pass it on. When we lose our self-awareness, we feel a sense of different from others in ways that cannot always be explained. The majority of people fear the things they do not know and, unfortunately, fear lies at the heart of many negative emotions. Being at peace with ourselves enables us to connect with the energy of others, to know intuitively

disconnection from everything and everyone. We live in a world of separation and fragmentation on every level. We base our identities on our roles within our jobs, families, communities, and even our race or religion. We feel their experiences without being consumed by them. Without a strong sense of self-belief, innate confidence, or self-love, we are vulnerable to being swept away by other people's energy in the form of intense will or emotional need.

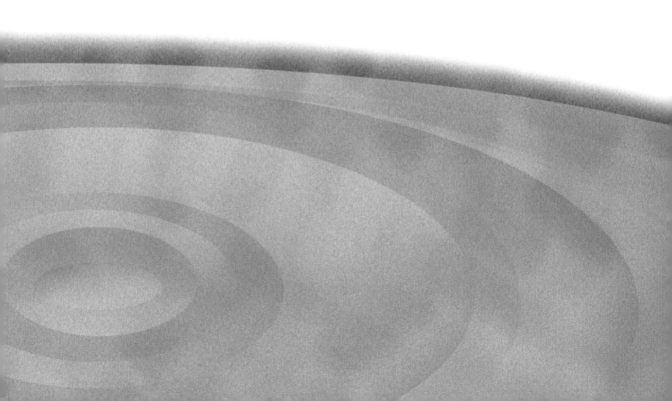

self-acceptance, or being **yourself**, is the first step to **mastering** your life

Opening ourselves to those around us is a vital aspect of personal growth. Self-awareness is particularly vital for establishing successful relationships with other people. It enables us to learn from and evaluate our experiences and

the experiences of others. We cannot know other people better than we know ourselves. We can only understand how other people may be feeling and thinking if we know our own thoughts and feelings. People who know themselves, and accept who they are, are much less likely to be selfish and much more likely to focus their energies on others. Self-awareness leads toward the capacity to take yourself, rather than others, for granted.

All of us have the ability to radiate positive energy. This happens when we are in touch with our emotions, confident and comfortable with our thoughts and beliefs, and able to transform negative feelings into a positive, life-enhancing lesson or step toward self-awareness. The energy of negative emotions can be channeled toward a goal when it is analyzed and accepted as something that be changed, or used as a tool toward understanding ourselves.

self-acceptance

People who do not accept themselves, who are negative or critical about their strengths, who cannot accept praise without feeling guilty, who do not see themselves as likeable, capable, or worthy to others are much more likely to be inward-centered. They are much more likely to dissipate the energies that could have gone into growth or building positive relationships, into worrying, self-rejection, and internal turbulence.

Self-acceptance, or being yourself, is the first step to mastering our lives. Self-accepting people are able to throw themselves into all kinds of activities with potential for self-expression and growth. Self-accepting people are also much more likely to accept other people and do the kind of things conducive to gaining acceptance from others. With self-acceptance comes self-belief, an essential ingredient for being able to interact successfully with others. Believe in and trust yourself. Love yourself and you will find that your rapport with others is markedly improved.

developing rapport

The ability to establish and maintain rapport is essential for good communication. People with a natural rapport unconsciously match each other's behavior and speech patterns. Neurolinguistic Programming (NLP) shows us how to create rapport in a more conscious way.

an image, directly right for a remembered sound, directly left for a constructed sound, down and to your right when having an internal dialogue with themselves, and down and left when experiencing feelings.

A person's thought process is very closely tied with their physiology. For example, a dog senses your fear, but how did he know if you didn't tell him? If a friend is depressed, most of us can tell without even talking to him. We pick up clues from his body—slumped head and shoulders, eyes downcast, and lack of animation. NLP looks for patterns in communication behavior. One of the earliest patterns noticed in humans was a tendency for the eyes to look in a particular direction when thinking in a certain way or about something specific. For example, people generally look up and to your right when thinking about a remembered image, up and left when constructing

This may seem complicated, but watching the face of the person to whom you are speaking can provide information about how he is thinking, which helps you decide what approach to take when communicating back to him.

To put NLP into action, match your words to the sensory system most indicated by the other person's actions. For example, if you ask someone a question and he turns his eyes to your immediate right or left, he is using auditory constructions (sounds and the sounds of words)

and will therefore respond best to aural cues. Saying, "I see what you mean" will probably not have the same effect as saying "I hear what you are saying." Auditory people need auditory cues, such as listen, hear, register, tune in, sound out, recall, verbalize, voice, and orchestrate.

MIRROR IMAGE

People with rapport have synchronized body language. They unconsciously seem to adopt similar postures, gestures, and eye movements. They may speak at more or less the same pace and even breathing patterns may be similar. If one person makes a movement, the other person may mirror it.

If someone turns his eyes up to the right or the left when he is thinking or responding, he is using visual constructions (pictures and images). He will therefore respond best to visual cues. Saying "I see what you mean" is therefore better than saying "I understand what you are feeling."

If you appeal to the visual—that is, provide a visual picture—you will be speaking the same language. For example, if you ask a colleague to prepare a report on the stacks of invoices in the box room, she will form an instant picture of the piles of papers and probably balk at the idea. If, however, you provide a visual strategy—tell her to box the invoices according to date, line them up against that wall, and work through them in order—your colleague will be more likely to respond better. She will be able to picture this scenario, which will be much more appealing than simply a vague sense of doing the task.

If the person with whom you are talking lowers his eyes down to the right side of his body, this indicates kinesthetic tendencies—body sensations, emotions, smell, and taste. To communicate best with this person you need to describe what you are feeling. "I feel good about the whole project," for example, or "I feel comfortable and happy with you in charge."

Recognizing whether people are seeing, hearing, or feeling allows you to match the sensory system they're using to communicate with them much more easily. If they use words such as look, see, appear, show, illustrate, if you appeal to the visual you will be speaking the same language

observe, focus, colorful, bright, clear, dull, dark, dim, or brilliant, they are probably thinking visually, so choose words of the same nature to communicate on the same level. If they use words such as listen, hear, register, ask, recall, verbalize, shrill, quit, loud, voice, or ask, they are probably thinking aurally, so use similar words, too. If words such as touch, feel, sense, grasp, drift, hold, catch, hit, firm, warm, smooth, cold, heavy, painful, soft, or sensuous are used, then this indicates a kinesthetic approach, and you will need to use the same kind of words when communicating back.

"I see what you are saying," "I hear you," "I understand," or "I sympathize"—use the right words and you will be much more likely to get through.

matching and pacing

Other ways of building a rapport involve matching and pacing. Matching is the art of adjusting aspects of your own external behavior and speech so it is similar to the other person's external behavior and speech.

what to match

- Body stance (feet apart or side by side, hands on hips, arms crossed, and so on)
- Hand gestures (opened palms, clenched fist)
- Facial gestures (wrinkled nose or raised eyebrows)
- Breathing rate
- Voice tone and pitch
- Vocal volume
- Speed of verbal delivery
- General rhythm and inflection of speech (length of gaps between phrases, emphasis on different words)
- Frequently repeated phrases or metaphors

When pacing the content of a conversation, respond to the words being said or the feelings and thoughts that are implied. Remember to respond, as opposed to react. If you are responsive, the other person experiences you as someone who is listening. Mirroring (see page 141) involves deliberately using body language to literally mirror the person to whom you are speaking.

Basically, matching and pacing involve identifying a pattern in the other person. Mirror that pattern and then subtly change the pattern. Observe with eyes and ears as to what happens. If the person does not follow you then resume the pace and try again momentarily. Match your body language if you want to get your message through. To check if your partner is matching, make small changes to your body language and watch if they are reflected.

Pacing lets people know, at an unconscious level, that you are willing to understand their model of the world—in other words, that you will listen to their story, see things from their point of view, and try to empathize or experience what they are feeling.

This is a fairly crude interpretation of the science of NLP, but one which can help you improve your communication skills. Remember that matching and mirroring have to be done as sensitively and as naturally as possible. If the person to whom you are speaking suspects mimicry or overt attempts to win them over, no rapport will be established. Remember, too, that "mismatching" can be a useful skill, particularly to close an exchange.

the art of body language

By changing the tone of voice we use for certain words, or by adjusting our body language slightly, we can give a completely different meaning to what we are saying. When

we communicate, it is important to be aware of the body language we display, and to ensure that it is congruent with our message. If you shift your eyes and look away a lot, people will not believe what you say. Similarly, making eye contact less than 50 percent of the time, shifting your weight from hip to hip, sighing, and fidgeting are all signs that you don't care about what someone is saying.

Do you stand with your shoulders back, walk with a lilt, make eye contact and smile? If you do, you will be seen as more forceful and energetic, more of a leader. If you walk with your shoulders slumped, keep your head down, speak in a flat tone, or fidget a lot, you will be seen as someone who can't make up his mind, is more negative, or needs a lot of guidance. Remember, how you are perceived is up to you.

the four basic modes of body language

responsive

engaged

leaning forward

open body

open arms

open hands

eager

open legs

feet under chair

on toes

leaning forward

ready to agree

closing papers

putting pen down

placing hands flat

    on table

reflective

listening

head tilted

lots of eye contact

nodding

high blink rate

evaluating

sucking glasses/pencil

stroking chin

looking up and right

crossing legs

    (ankle on knee)

attentive

standing with arms

    behind back

smiling

feet open and apart

fugitive

bored

staring into space

slumped posture

doodling

tapping foot

wanting to go

feet facing toward door

looking around

buttoning jacket

rejection

sitting/moving back

folding arms

crossing legs

    (thigh on knee)

putting head down

frowning

defensive

standing with feet

    pointing inward

clenching hands

combative

let me speak

finger tapping

foot tapping

staring

aggressive

leaning forward

finger pointing

fists clenched

defiant

standing with hands

    on hips

frowning

lying

touching face

hand over mouth

pulling ear

eyes cast downward

glancing at you

shifting in seat

looking down and left

reading body language

According to the book by Allan Pease, *Body Language: How to Read Other's Thoughts by Their Gestures*, body language is universal and can be learned and used, both to read the feelings and attitudes of the people with whom we communicate, and as a tool to communicate better with our own bodies. Remember to read body language as a series of patterns; a single gesture can mean nothing. You will soon build up a picture of what's going on by assessing the stance, eye movements, and other behavior exhibited by the person with whom you are communicating.

some common gestures

- Open palms signify honesty and openness.
- Palms up signifies submissiveness, palms down signifies domination, closed fist represents aggression.
- Rubbing palms indicates positive expectation. Done quickly, it suggests mutual benefit. Done slowly, it suggests deviousness and self-interest.
- A thumb and finger rub is done in expectation of income.
- People will sometimes try to dominate a handshake by excessively squeezing and shaking, or by rotating the hand grip so that their hand is uppermost. The opposite can also also occur.
- To offer a hand for shaking when it is not desired can be pushy and offensive.
- Hand clenching may indicate frustration.
- Holding your own hand behind your back exposes your front and shows you are confident. Taking this position is useful during stressful situations.
- Putting fingers in pockets but keeping thumbs out can indicate confidence or domination.

- Pointing with a thumb and fist is derogatory.
- Hand to face gestures (mouth guarding/nose touching/eye rubbing) can indicate deceit if they occur in clusters.
- Neck touching may indicate dishonesty without conviction. Asking for clarification may reveal the truth.
- Lip touching or finger sucking may indicate nervousness.
- Supporting the head with the hand can indicate boredom.
- Chin stroking indicates evaluation.
- Spectacle adjusting or cigarette handling can indicate evaluation and uncertainty, and a desire for time to think before responding.
- A folded arm across the chest suggests nervousness, defensiveness, or a negative attitude. It can be used to block an unpleasant idea.
- Women who hold a handbag at their chest may be using it and one or both arms as a barrier to ideas.
- Men may adjust their watches or shirt buttons to disguise a barrier to ideas. Legs may be used as barriers, especially when seated.
- Lint picking may be a sign of disagreement.

- A head tilt indicates interest and/or curiosity.
- Relaxing in the presence of others indicates calm equality.
- Hand on hips indicates readiness or aggression.
- Leaning forward when seated indicates readiness (to agree or to leave).
- Contracted pupils are negative and can indicate anger.
- Dilated pupils indicate excitement (regular or sexual).
- Too little eye contact may indicate dishonesty or nerves.
- Too much eye contact may indicate hostility.
- Looking at another's forehead during a business discussion can help maintain control.
- Looking at another's nose or mouth is more social.
- If someone keeps closing their eyes while talking to you, it may indicate that they don't want to see you.

male courtship gestures

■ Preening (hair smoothing, tie straightening).

■ Hand near or pointing to genitals.

■ Body facing female or foot pointing toward female.

■ Eye contact.

■ Giving the "intimate gaze," (looking from a woman's eyes to her chest).

■ Pupil dilation (if very keen).

■ A readiness position (body leaning forward or placing hands on hips).

■ Wide leg stance.

female courtship gestures

■ Blushing.

■ Tossing head to flick back hair.

■ Exposing or displaying wrists.

■ Rolling hips.

■ Glancing sideways, possibly over a raised shoulder.

■ Open mouth.

■ Wet lips.

■ Fondling objects.

■ Pointing with knee.

■ Fondling shoe with foot.

other gestures

- People who show off cars (or partners) will lean against or touch them to display ownership.
- People who agree with each other during a discussion will often adopt similar positions. If one person's body language is consistently repeated by the other, then that person is the strong one, the "leader" in the relationship.
- People may stand on something to make themselves look more important. Conversely, they may stoop to show submission. This can be helpful if you have to invade someone's territory and want to avoid confrontation.
- People point their body toward what they are interested in. If a person's body isn't facing yours during a discussion, they may not be interested.
- Two people talking, but looking the same way, may indicate openness to being joined by someone from the direction they are looking.

actions speak louder than words

It is actually impossible not to communicate. Even if you
refrain from speaking, you are still communicating non-
verbally through facial expressions and body language. If you
decide, for example, not to attend a meeting or are late

meeting a friend, you are still communicating.
All of us should consider that our actions speak volumes,
and that we are continuously faced with decisions that
communicate information about ourselves, our intentions,
and feelings about others.

At all times, therefore, you should be mindful about what you want to communicate. If you do not clearly define and take charge of what, when, and how you communicate, you can easily be misunderstood or misinterpreted. You leave yourself completely open to the assumptions of others. Trust, of course, plays a large part in the communication equation. If you work or live with people who understand your motives, know that you are responsible, and feel comfortable with you as a colleague or team member, the assumptions about you will be positive. If those same people are insecure within themselves, or about you, they may make assumptions that serve their own best interests. Until trust is secured in any relationship, it is best to state your intentions, clarify your position, and broadcast your motives. It is also important to teach people how to treat you by setting clear boundaries. Communicating proactively prevents false assumptions by others.

Remember, too, that there unspoken rules about communication. For example, what we say isn't necessarily what the other person hears. You need to learn the art of matching your body language to the words you are saying, and to repeat and reinforce your message constantly, requesting, if necessary, that the other person summarizes your conversation. People have a tendency to hear what they want to hear, and the foundation of mistrust and misinterpretation is often based on this premise. What they do hear is, ultimately, more important than what we say, because this is the message we have communicated. Be sure you know that the message you intended was received. Similarly, many conversations are not understood, are incomplete, or send contrary (but not intentional) messages just by the words or tone used to express the thought.

mental rehearsal

Just as an actor prepares for a play by rehearsing his lines in a scene, we can all learn better communication skills through practice. In personal development psychology, mental rehearsal is a subset of practices known collectively as mental rehearsal skills. They include visualization, affirmations, and controlled self-talk, including the use of "power language" (in other words, vocabulary which has a powerful biochemical and physiological effect, such as "the best," "the greatest," "the fastest," and so on).

We all "go through in our minds" how we think we are likely to perform in forthcoming situations or conversations, but this is slightly different from mental rehearsal. Mental rehearsal is a matter of recalling the precise actions in sequence, getting the mental syntax right.

When we learn the art of communicating, we feel confident enough to enter into discussions and conversations, and hold our own. Before we reach that zenith, however, it does pay to mentally rehearse. Plan in advance the message you wish to get across, and picture yourself holding a successful conversation. Use positive visualization techniques to imagine both yourself speaking, and others listening. Focus on your words, your body language, your gestures, and your facial expressions.

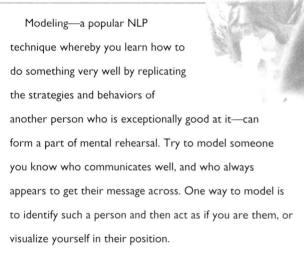

Modeling—a popular NLP technique whereby you learn how to do something very well by replicating the strategies and behaviors of another person who is exceptionally good at it—can form a part of mental rehearsal. Try to model someone you know who communicates well, and who always appears to get their message across. One way to model is to identify such a person and then act as if you are them, or visualize yourself in their position.

Once you've mastered the art of communicating your vision, feelings, and beliefs, you may only need to practice mental rehearsal for tricky situations, but it's a useful tool to have on standby.

conflict and confrontation

Communication skills provide you with the tools you need to manage conflict, which gives you a sense of control in your relationships at home, with friends, and in the office. Studies show that employees are more productive when their ideas are listened to and acted upon. They will go the extra mile when their feelings are validated. The same holds true for personal relationships.

The first step in creating a strong rapport is to offer a "support statement." This is an acknowledgment of someone else's needs, such as "I understand that you always find this type of project difficult," or "I realise that you are feeling unhappy with my working hours." A support statement begins a conversation in a positive and empathetic way, validating concerns and creating trust.

No matter how well you learn the art of communicating, there will always be times when you reach loggerheads, or come up against "problem people."

First and foremost in any conflict, you must remember that problems seemingly caused by other people, and therefore beyond your control, can actually be solved by changes in your own behavior. This works surprisingly well because other people's behavior toward you consists largely of reactions to your behavior. This doesn't mean compromising your position or your values, it simply means considering how you are putting yourself across.

the victim mentality

A false belief that you are a victim and have no control of a situation may lead you to believe that you are being treated unfairly. Remember that the way people react to you is strongly affected by your behavior toward them. If they are critical of you, try unilaterally changing your behavior so that their criticism becomes impossible. Discover and control habits that other people may find annoying. Try to chip away at their behavioral problems by changing your own behavior in ways that may encourage them to modify theirs—be extra nice to someone who has insulted you or offer an olive branch to someone who has never had any time for you.

no autonomy

If your self-worth is based on the opinions of others, you will tend to be drawn into relationships where your need for others' approval puts you into helpless situations. To recondition your own behavior toward self-actualization, try to set up experiences where you accomplish things simply to please yourself. If you concentrate on building up your own self-esteem, you will find that you are better able to communicate your thoughts and feelings because you feel in control, and justifiably firm in your own self-belief.

All of us have the ability to alter our behavior and that of those around us in such a way that we can tackle our problems more successfully and achieve a complete solution. Problems tend to arise because we continue with a certain course of action, or maintain certain views and attitudes that create negative or unpleasant experiences. Look at your expectations. You might expect positive, pleasant, and agreeable encounters in all areas of your life, but you must be prepared for times when conflict rears its head.

problem people

While most of us share a decorum of respect and consideration for other people, there are those who, for some reason, can't seem to control themselves and have the ability to make parts of our lives a misery. Dr. Kerry L. Johnson, an American business psychologist and

motivational speaker, has come up with a list of problem types and tips on how best to deal with them. Handling a problem person takes a lot of skill and, more importantly, courage. One of the central coping techniques is to stand up to these people. Most of us avoid conflict so much that we ignore or walk away from these types. When problem people aren't confronted, they tend to repeat the bad behavior because it works for them. If you are firm and assertive, and use the techniques outlined, you may not be able to avoid problem people, but you'll be able to defuse them by coping, rather than fighting or withdrawing.

THE BULLDOZER

These people are frequently seen as intimidating. They walk into a room and make people shudder. Their goal is to get their own way at any cost. But their bad behavior seems to be successful only in the short run. It is rarely long-term. They are very focused in their obsession to win every argument. In fact, they seem good at storing up facts to use in their argumentative attacks. This gives them immense power in manipulating others.

The way to deal with bulldozers is to sit them down immediately. It's usually harder to maintain anger when one is sitting. In many cases, that's all it takes. Since the bulldozer is often an emotional bully, if you confront them head on, they may realize quickly that the altercation is getting out of hand. Otherwise, ask them a few questions about their problem. Listen carefully without accusing them of bad behavior, as this may just inflame them even more. Draw them into a conversation as this may help diffuse their outburst into a more constructive discussion.

Look bulldozers directly in the eye and respond assertively without emotion, instead of aggressively. If they interrupt you (which they most likely will) cut them off by saying, "Just a moment, you'll get your turn." But don't let them continue to bulldoze you.

THE SNIPER

These are the sort who talk about you behind your back. They make little jokes or quip about your weaknesses. Since they shoot from the cover of innocent humor, others don't see the viciousness of their hostility. Snipers rob you of your self-esteem, like other hostile-aggressives. But unlike the loud and abusive sort, they do it surreptitiously. Since there is so much peer pressure to take a joke in good humor, snipers often get away with embarrassing comments without any fear of reprisal. They rarely attack openly due to their perceived loss of cover. They'd rather attack you under the camouflage of wit and humor.

One way to deal with a sniper is to avoid responding to comments made anonymously. If you are attacked in front of others with wit as a typical camouflage, ignore the sniper. He or she is hoping you will laugh at yourself so you can be sniped at in good fun yet again.

Ask snipers about their comments when they are alone. Ask if their nasty comments were meant as a dig. They are very likely to say, "What's the matter? Can't you take a little joke?" Respond with, "Sure I can. But I sensed a little animosity behind your comments. Is that the way you meant to say it?" If they say yes, you have a chance to discover what the real irritation is behind the comment.

THE VOLCANO

Human volcanoes erupt without provocation but seem most explosive under pressure. Like bulldozers, they are hostile-aggressive in nature, but blow up out of control. Their mode of operation is to first blame a problem on another and then explode. The episode is usually caused by the volcano's low level of self-esteem and overall feeling of being threatened. Ways to deal with a volcano include letting them talk until they run down, the way a wind-up toy loses its energy. If you listen well when a spouse or colleague is upset, problems will often solve themselves.

Another way is to tell them that you wish to hear what they are upset about, but not in this way. On the telephone interrupt them by saying, "Hang on, I want to get a pen and paper to jot some notes down as you talk." Get as many facts as possible about their concerns. Focus on the tangible details as a way to deflect the emotion.

Ways to deal with conflict:

1 Change your behavior in a way that puts you in a better position.

2 Withdraw from situations that do nothing for you in the long run.

3 Avoid people and conditions that are likely to do you harm.

Analyze your attitude to discover if you are actually the cause of the conflict. If you can see nothing in your behavior that could be construed as offensive or challenging, stand by your values and work on making them clear in an unchallenging way. Your needs and wishes are important, and you should not feel that you need to give way to others in order to preserve the peace.

when we communicate with others
we run the risk of being rejected

dealing with rejection

When we communicate with others we always run the risk of being rejected. Confidence and self-belief can be damaged when we open ourselves up to potential hurt, but rejection and conflict are part of life, and we must learn to deal with them. When we are rejected, it is essential that we reclaim a positive sense of self. We can also avoid setting ourselves up for rejection by being honest and communicative, and ensuring that others are aware that we are speaking from the heart. It takes a very callous person to inflict hurt on someone who is emotionally honest and aware.

If you do find yourself in the position of being rejected, take time to acknowledge your hurt. Take it out and examine it. Why does it hurt so much? What hopes did you have attached to this particular form of acceptance? It is how we interpret, internalize, and react to events that brings us joy or pain. It is how we see ourselves in relation to others around us. The greater your sense of self-worth, and the stronger your self-esteem, the more able you are to bounce back from rejection.

Do you look for a reflection of yourself in the eyes of others? If someone else finds you unlikeable, irritating, or unlovable, it does not mean that your cover has been blown and you have been revealed as someone not worth loving. Continue to love yourself—do things that make you feel good about yourself. Bolster your self-esteem by doing something that you do well. Surround yourself with people who nurture you, and who enjoy your company.

Self-worth should not be based on other people's opinions of you. You cannot be all things to all people. You can only be yourself. If that's good enough for most people in your life, you can be satisfied there is nothing real to worry about.

Have realistic expectations. If someone has always treated you a certain way in the past, why do you keep hoping that this time will be different? Stop hurting yourself by expecting them to change and accept the situation for what it is. You cannot change others—you can only change yourself. Ask yourself, "How can I change my behavior and respond to their behavior in a more positive manner?"

Don't be tempted to close down and suppress your feelings. Suppressing your feelings will only cause them to stagnate, and exaggerate the importance of the episode in the context of your life. Instead, be honest with yourself. Evaluate your own needs, and recognize that there will always be times when your self-value is challenged. Look at negative experiences as a lesson or challenge. Express yourself to the rejecter, and make it clear how you are feeling. Find the strength within you to draw a line under the episode, relationship, or situation, and trust that you have the courage to move forward.

the art of negotiation

Negotiating involves great self-assurance, and an ability to communicate clearly and confidently. There is an art to negotiation, and it helps to ensure that everyone comes away feeling that they have won to some degree.

Be aware of intimidation tactics. Negative comments about your appearance or interrupting negotiations to take calls are common tactics to throw you off. If you are aware of this, you can dismiss them and focus on the job at hand.

Never overpower or intimidate your opposition, but avoid, too, the trap of falling into "nice guy/best friend." While you have a better chance of achieving your goals if you are liked, you shouldn't let that get in the way of the negotiating process. You can be strong and still be courteous.

Acknowledge this behavior to defuse confrontation and to help prevent a recurrence. Or, deflect the attack, but don't counterattack. Remember, you are in control of your emotions, not the other person. Be cool and witty. If you are kept waiting, for example, say, "You're obviously very distracted today, and I wouldn't want to take advantage of your inattention. Let's reschedule." If you value yourself and your time, and make that clear, they will have to follow suit.

Work on your communication skills. Ask open-ended questions rather than issue pronouncements. Be careful when using the word "why," though, because it can be perceived as accusatory. Invite discussion, and be open to

Most importantly, ooze the confidence that you feel inside. Don't let yourself become distracted from your purpose. Calm persistence is the most effective negotiating tool, as is an ability to empathize—that is, see and express

correction and persuasion. "Please correct me if I'm wrong . . . " or "Help me to understand . . . " are much more likely to spur the negotiating process and give you valuable information than some pronouncement from your position platform. Analyze and improve upon ideas from the opposition's point of view. Ask their advice. When in doubt, use silence. It makes most people very uncomfortable. Just remember, he who speaks first loses.

things from the opposition's point of view. Just as you would in a personal relationship, offer a support statement (see page 156), which establishes a willingness to settle things in an amicable and mutually beneficial way.

maintaining lasting relationships

Communication is the key to every healthy relationship, from those in the office through to family and other personal associations. In relationships, everyone has rights, and it is just as important to protect your own rights as it is to acknowledge and support the other's.

Everyone has the right to:

- Say I don't know.
- Say no.
- Have an opinion and express it.
- Have feelings and express them.
- Make their own decisions and deal with the consequences.
- Change their minds.
- Choose how to spend their time.
- Make mistakes.

We also need to learn the skill of assertiveness (which differs greatly from aggression), based on the idea that your needs, wants, and feelings are neither more nor less important than those of other people—they are equally important. You should, therefore, make claims for yourself appropriately, honestly, and clearly. Learning how to do this means that you do not come away from situations feeling bad about yourself, or leaving others feeling unhappy.

If you value yourself and trust your own feelings, you will express yourself to others effectively. What's more, you will find that people trust and value you more if you assert yourself and are honest. People who constantly take the role of doormat, or give in too easily, seem somehow less trustworthy. Be clear about your expectations and your wants. For example, saying "I want an early night tonight" is much better than making vague statements about being tired. It is not selfish to show that you have needs. It is selfish not to communicate them, as you will be operating with some dishonesty.

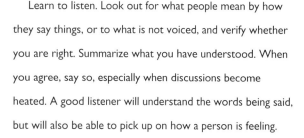

Learn to listen. Look out for what people mean by how they say things, or to what is not voiced, and verify whether you are right. Summarize what you have understood. When you agree, say so, especially when discussions become heated. A good listener will understand the words being said, but will also be able to pick up on how a person is feeling.

Try to cooperate. Look at the situation from other people's point of view—whether you are in harmony or discord. Risk saying how you feel and talking about what you want. Show you believe what other people say. Leave them the space they need to be their own person. Never avoid thorny issues. Understand that people need different amounts of closeness, silence to think or let off steam, sharing, independence, and physical contact.

Finally, cut out the blame. Instead of blaming others for the symptoms or feelings you are experiencing, ask yourself "What is in me that makes me feel this way?" When you find it, communicate it and keep the door wide open.

self-talk

Self-communication is as important as communication with the world around us. It keeps us in touch with ourselves, shapes our self-concept, our beliefs, and influences our feelings and all aspects of our behavior. And the best part

of coming to know ourselves, becoming our own "soulmate," is that we always have someone to whom we can turn when the outside world seems hostile. Self-talk is the basis of change. In other words, rather than trying to change our behavior directly, we can use self-talk to program our subconscious to bring about the changes we want. It is also the foundation of self-acceptance. When we get to know ourselves, beneath the babble of our everyday thoughts, we become comfortable with what we find there, and know that we can find within ourselves the strength, the determination, and the potential to be whatever we want to be.

Self-talk should be as honest and rewarding as interaction with anyone else. It involves showing empathy and understanding, and stifling the internal critic. Self-love depends upon self-acceptance, and we need to analyze and come to terms with all aspects of ourselves—our feelings, our behavior, our goals, ambitions, weaknesses, strengths, and insecurities. Take the time to be alone with yourself, to uncover the person you really are. Positive self-talk is essential. Always avoid phrases that the subconscious interprets as negatives—"I am hopeless at relationships," "I can't," or "I am no good"—and use instead positive affirmations to reinforce your self-image and self-belief. What you say when you talk to yourself is almost always a message you received from others, and according to behavioral psychologists, the vast majority of self-talk is negative, or works against you. Negative self-talk, such as "I'm too shy," or "It's just no use," causes you to doubt, be unsure, worry, and lack confidence.

Some ways to change your self-talk include listening to your self-talk, listening to the self-talk of others, rephrasing your negative self-talk to make it positive, and making your own self-talk to help you with problem areas. Positive self-

talk gives you strong new messages to help you overcome long-time fears and obstacles. It helps you to speak more comfortably in front of groups, become more confident around others, and look, act, and feel more in control. Renew your relationship with yourself today and extend your newfound confidence to the outside world.

the power of self-talk

In 1991, sports psychologists Lydia Ievleva and Terry Orlick, conducted a study into how self-talk affects the healing process of sports-related injuries. They discovered that those who engaged in positive self-talk had a much quicker recovery time than those who were negative and unforgiving. Positive self-talk statements included those such as "I can do it," and "I can recover sooner than normal," while negative self-talk involved remarks such as "It will take forever to get better." Research also shows that there is a definite link between negative self-talk and depression, anxiety, and psychosomatic symptoms. Conversely, people who use positive cognitive coping mechanisms displayed lower levels of depression and anxiety.

the effective you

The changes we make in our lives as a result of learning to understand, getting to know, and liking ourselves have a direct impact on the way we operate in the world. Increased self-esteem and self-respect provide the confidence we need to become more effective in all our relationships, and we are able to attain that elusive goal—happiness—because we have the tools to achieve whatever we want and be who we want to be.

When we are self-aware, we make time for things that make us feel good about ourselves. We treat ourselves with the respect we deserve, and that healthy mental attitude shines out into the world around us.

In this book, we have identified and begun the process of coming to terms with ourselves—our strengths and weaknesses, our abilities and shortcomings, and our infinite capacity to recognize and achieve our full potential. In this final chapter we'll look at how to maintain the equilibrium, keeping our mind and body fresh, and adapting to the challenges that life presents to find peace in our daily existence.

total health

Emotional health is inextricably linked to physical health. When we feel good emotionally—stable and in control—we feel healthier and are less susceptible to illness. Making the changes outlined in this book will positively affect your physical health, and inspire you to continue taking better care of your body. We treat people that we respect with care and kindness. When we become our own best friend, we find that we actually want to look after ourselves. We develop the confidence to believe that we matter, too.

Total, or holistic, health can be achieved by learning to listen to our bodies—recognizing the signs of imbalance and understanding when we need to slow down, seek stimulation, change our diets, take more exercise, or get more sleep.

In the hours you spend alone with yourself, take the time to assess your health and well-being. Use your newly developed insight and intuition to recognize when all is not well, and where changes should be made. Meditate on your body. Just as you have learned to get to know your emotional and innermost self, so, too, can you get to know your physical self. Become aware of how you move and carry yourself. You body mirrors your state of mind. Observe your body language with objectivity and learn to understand it. What is your body expressing now? Joy or burden? Worry or peace? Fear or freedom? Are you carrying tension? Are you relaxed?

Start thinking about your physical well-being by asking yourself the following questions:

■ Do you sleep well?

■ Do you have reserves of stamina and energy that allow you to achieve what you want from your life?

■ Do you have any recurring minor illnesses, such as coughs or colds?

■ Do you exercise regularly?

■ Is your diet balanced and healthy?

■ Do you have any addictive habits, such as smoking or drinking to excess?

■ Do you take the time you need to relax?

Reflect on your answers and consider making positive changes toward your overall health and well-being.

Your ability to communicate and sustain healthy relationships is an important part of your emotional well-being. Pause now to consider your emotional health. Ask yourself if:

■ You are able to make and maintain long-term friendships and relationships.

■ You are a good friend, parent, partner, or child, and if you are able to achieve this naturally and not through a misguided sense of loyalty or guilt.

■ You can express feelings of love and tenderness to others.

■ You can deal with anger.

■ You can accept forgiveness, and are able to forgive yourself and others.

If you find areas of weak emotional health, resolve to make changes. Begin by liking yourself. When you are at peace with yourself, you will find it easier to share your happiness and joy with those around you.

According to Dr. Tony Humphreys, an Irish consultant clinical psychologist, we all have basic needs that must be met (see opposite), and it's important that we regularly take the time to assess them.

Responding to your needs in a regular and active way is a major part of the unconditional relationship you have with yourself. Neglecting this responsibility only serves to weaken your value and sense of self.

A love of life is a strong indicator of high self-esteem. A person with middle to low self-esteem avoids challenge as the risk of failure is too threatening. When you take on challenges, you get in touch with the power to take responsibility for your own life. Avoiding change as a way of protecting yourself from hurt and humiliation keeps your self-esteem at a low level.

Choices about change can only be made in the present, which means that it is important to accept where you are now. Therefore, the first condition for fruitful change is seeing clearly where you are at the moment. Do not hide away from present reality. If there are aspects of the present you do not like, plan how to change them. If you pretend these aspects do not exist, you will never change them. At times you will want to make energetic and active changes, exerting your will to direct or control forces around you. At others times, a quieter, more accepting form of change may provide what you need, steering you away from turbulent waters into calmer ones. The potential for change in the future can only live in the present.

basic human needs

- Emotional: love, affection, warmth, closeness, understanding, support, and humor.
- Physical: health, fitness, comfort, safety, food, and warmth.
- Social: friendship, companionship, sharing of expertise, knowledge, and experience.
- Cognitive: intellectual challenge and responsibility.
- Behavioral: the development of a broad range of skills, for example, writing, gardening, cooking, or woodworking.
- Sensual: all five senses need adequate stimulation.
- Occupational: meaningful, recognized work, fair salary and conditions, benefits, and promotional prospects.
- Sexual: gratification of a sexual drive within the context of a mature and loving relationship.
- Recreational: rest, games, sports, hobbies, and interests.
- Spiritual: personal or organized religious exploration of our spiritual nature.

the importance of humor

Life is not all order and joy, nor is it all pain and chaos. The human experience can be enjoyed regardless of what may be in your life at any given time. Learning to see

life through a humorous filter does not guarantee that we won't have some pain, disappointment, or failure. Rather, it ensures that we are not destroyed in the process. We need to recapture the joy, excitement, and wonder of our childhood. Taking yourself, your career, business, problems, or life in general too seriously contributes to leading a life filled with pain and anxiety.

Science has proven that laughter massages the internal organs, enhancing digestion and circulation. Humor also releases endorphins in the brain that give us an overall sense of well-being.

seeing the absurd allows for freedom of thought

what is humor?

Humor is the ability to recognize the absurd in any situation and to accept it. Humor is the ability not to take yourself or others too seriously. Lightheartedness is the

essence of a joyful and creative life. A sense of mirth helps to relax the mind and make it more flexible. Humor can also be cultivated and developed. As your creative abilities increase, you sense the absurd in any situation, which allows for freedom of thought.

Look for humor in everyday life—people who are doing amusing things, anything that might make you laugh. The more you look, the more you will find. Even if you don't particularly feel like laughing, try it once in a while anyway. The reflexes, smile, and physiological changes your body undergoes make you feel better almost immediately.

Aim to inject humor into tense situations—it is a useful tool for dispersing stress and helps everyone to relax. Studies show that following laughter, the body is calmer, the brain is clearer, and many physical health problems are alleviated. You may also be more capable of solving problems that seemed impossible a few minutes before.

And finally, always try to start off each day with a smile. Use your smile to establish a positive attitude that lets you make the most of each day.

setting attainable goals

Life moves forward regardless of whether we resist or flow with it. Clear, focused, and worthwhile goals keep you moving in the right direction toward higher ground.

Resolve, each day, to find your passion and purpose, and become better, wiser, and stronger. This will guarantee the peace you desire, the success you deserve, and the happiness you search for. Dream big goals and don't let anyone discourage you. Set your goals, take action on them, and watch your future unfold as you have dreamed.

Imagine that you work for a company and you have reached the end of your financial year. You have accomplished everything in your personal and professional life that you have set out to do. What do you see? What is your life like? Ask yourself how you feel, now that you have achieved your dreams. Why do you want these things?

Create a mental picture of what life is like at this future state. Try then to create something physical—a list, painting, collage—anything that represents your ideal position in life. This is your vision picture. Keep it on your desk or refrigerator, anywhere that reminds you daily of what you wish to achieve in the future.

Break your vision down into a list of personal and professional goals. Make sure your goals are specific and realistic. Attach deadlines to your goals so you can keep pace and make the proper adjustments to stay on track.

Determine what the key activities and responsibilities are that will move you most swiftly to your goals. Then organize your schedule around these first and foremost.

Let your vision motivate, pull, and guide you toward your desired future state. Use your imagination and your new self-belief to ensure that you stay on track. If you put yourself in a resourceful state, you can access your perseverance, self-confidence, enthusiasm, and self-motivation. Use positive thinking to reinforce your goals and regularly remind yourself why they make you happy. The journey to reaching your goals should always be pleasurable. If it is not, ask yourself whether the goals you have set are realistic and in tune with your needs. Don't be afraid to make changes. Relax into the belief that you can be anything and anywhere you want to be.

finding your outlet

An overly rigid approach to setting and achieving goals can prohibit the natural flow of energy, creativity, and thought. While goals are crucial to moving forward in our lives, it is important to remember that success is a journey, not a destination. We must enjoy the process of achieving our dreams, as well as the end result.

One of the most important ways of ensuring that we are on the right path is to set up a series of self-checks. Every so often, honestly appraise how you are feeling. Ask yourself,

"Which areas in my life are providing me with the most pleasure?" "What parts of my life are incomplete or unsatisfactory?" To do this, you need to create an outlet from your life, a little space from the continual grind of everyday living. Time alone is essential for the self-learning process and important for self-monitoring. But you also need to engage in something that releases energy, clears the channels, and invigorates the body and mind. No time for play and relaxation can create both emotional and physical stress, which affects overall health and well-being.

Find time to let off steam, to allow your natural buoyant energy and spirit to unfold. Let down your defenses and let out all that energy that has been bubbling inside during the day. Organize some fun exercise. Spend a day outdoors running and exploring. See the world around you as though you were a child again. Laugh, joke, wrestle, play—anything that lets your energy glow in a natural way. Be exuberant— shout, cheer, cry. Or just daydream, lying back in the sun contemplating your surroundings, which you are often too busy to see. Seek the beauty in life—in the small, the everyday, and the insignificant. Look at things with fresh eyes.

Taking time to let off steam will help you clear your mind, clarify your energy, and encourage you to develop your innate ability to find peace within yourself. You will be refreshed and able to look at things with a different perspective. Use your sharpened intuition to ask yourself if the path you are taking is the right one for you. If it's not, don't be afraid to make changes.

learning to relax

Science has been late in discovering that mind and body function as a complete, working unit. It is a long-held belief of Eastern philosophers and holistic medical practitioners,

Relaxation is an essential part of a healthy lifestyle and intrinsic to happiness. When relaxed, we experience more of life because we have the patience and ability to find pleasure in everyday things. We are not bogged down by the minutiae of achieving success, meeting goals, and sticking to a predefined path. We feel physically well, which allows us to experience emotional and spiritual well-being. Tension not only damages the body, it also cramps the mind and the capacity to enjoy our lives.

but only the new science of psychoneuroimmunology has convinced the medical establishment that mental activity has a direct effect on the body, and that the reverse is also true, particularly with regard to stress and relaxation.

Research has shown that relaxation reduces adrenaline levels and allows the immune system to function more efficiently. This is because the body's two defense mechanisms—the alarm and immune systems—work together to ensure our survival. The alarm system is the body's fight-or-flight reaction, which is mobilized by stress. It responds quickly to stressors, increasing adrenaline levels to make us run away from a threat or stand and fight it. When the threat has passed, adrenaline levels return to normal. However, if we are under constant stress, they rarely get the chance. As a result, the body feels as if it is under constant attack. This feeling of constant pressure has a wearing effect on our immune system, which protects us from disease and relies on good nutrition and a positive mental attitude. An alarm system on constant alert overstimulates the immune system so that it can no longer distinguish between real and presumed threats, allowing disease to take hold. Scientists are researching the belief that and does little apart from take the weight off your feet. The stresses of the day—the criticisms, disappointments, and anger—stay locked in the body, causing anxiety, frustration,

one of the most powerful influences on the immune system may in fact be our view of how well we cope with stress. Stress is a normal and necessary part of life. It does not go away, so it must be controlled. Controlled stress provides motivation, stimulation, and the drive to meet challenges with enthusiasm. The key to controlling stress is relaxation. For many of us, this involves lying on the settee watching television at the end of a long day. This form of passive relaxation has no therapeutic benefits

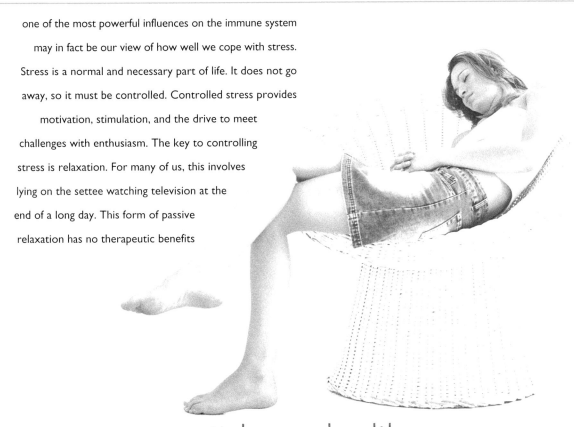

relaxation is an essential part of a healthy lifestyle

depression in the mind, and tension in the muscles and ligaments of the body. True relaxation is a healing process that focuses on relaxing the mind and body. It involves turning your attention inward to control and resolve the effects of stress, rather than suppressing those effects with short-term measures, such as drugs, cigarettes, and alcohol.

all the other negative emotions threatening our peace of mind and physical health. Prepare for meditation (see page 34), and breathe slowly and deeply. Do not rush the

Relaxation is a skill. Practiced correctly, it is an important factor in preventing disease on every level—from the general feeling of ease and well-being that increases when adrenaline levels are lowered, to fighting off the common cold and even reducing the risk of developing life-threatening illness, such as cancer. Mental well-being is enhanced by relaxation. Alertness and concentration can be improved, and memory and creativity are boosted. Above all, relaxation means that people are less dependent upon artificial sedatives, such as tranquilizers, antidepressants, and hypnotic drugs. Relaxation provides time out from the turmoil and chaos around us, a chance for the human body and spirit to recharge its batteries.

Make time for relaxation in every day—not passive relaxation involving distractions, but activities that free the body and mind from tension, competition, worry, fear, and

relaxation experience. It is an important part of achieving harmony in your mind and body, and helps you to tackle life's challenges, as well as embrace the purpose of your ultimate journey—happiness.

Repeat the following words to yourself as you feel the tension release on each exhale:

- The muscles of my head and face are relaxing. I am feeling relaxed.
- The muscles of my neck are relaxing. I am feeling relaxed.
- The muscles of my shoulders and chest are relaxing. I am relaxed.
- The muscles of my arms and hands are relaxing.
- The muscles of my legs are relaxing. I am very relaxed.
- I feel relaxed. My mind is calm.
- My body is calm. I am very relaxed.

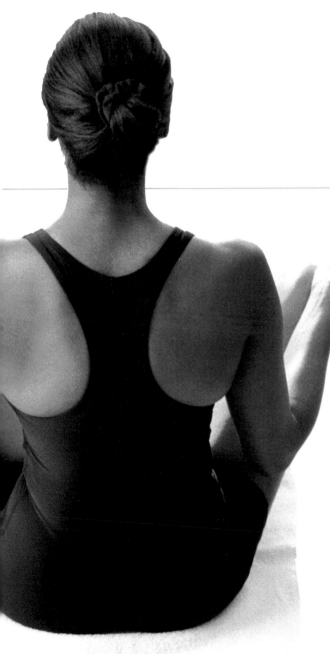

dealing with everyday setbacks

We often describe setbacks as being "soul-destroying." The reason for this may be because they threaten our fragile self-confidence, our belief in ourselves, and the knowledge that we can be whatever we want to be. They undermine our spirit and disrupt our inner peace. But only if we let them.

Problems and setbacks are an unfortunate part of life.

To deal with them, it is essential that you avoid holding a fixed view of how things should be. Setbacks can often mean disappointment, but they may also present new challenges and provoke change when least expected. Rather than ruing your altered expectations, learn to accept what comes your way, and try not to fix the outcome of future events. Don't hide your feelings—discuss them, work through them, and analyze them to help you overcome your anxiety, fear, and confusion. Use meditation to keep you focused on the present. In any case, goals are never set in stone—they should shift and alter according to the things you find out about yourself as you travel on your journey. Always focus on today, on achieving happiness in the here and now, and within yourself. You will regain your self-confidence and be able to meet the challenges of tomorrow with renewed vigor.

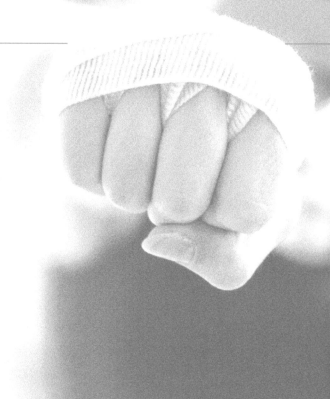

happiness and integrity

Self-observation will tell you where you are today, and how you are feeling. Continually test yourself to work out how you are feeling, how you are doing, and whether you are

really happy with the way your life is unfolding. Go back to Chapter 1 and do the all exercises again. Who are you now? Has your vision of yourself changed? Look again at the qualities that you consider to be negative, and ask yourself whether they matter as much.

The process of self-awareness and learning to like yourself is ever-changing, so self-monitor regularly to pinpoint your strengths and weaknesses, and to find the areas of your life you can change. Every day you have choices to make—not just life-changing decisions, but small things that will affect how you feel about yourself, others, and the world around you. Every choice you make brings an opportunity to behave, think, react, or respond through self-awareness. Do you make the most of every opportunity?

Always tell the truth. Truth creates intimacy with the self. To experience intimacy with others, you must first learn to be intimate with yourself. When you can face

Being successful requires high self-esteem and self-respect. What does it really take to develop a level of self-esteem that not only radiates success, but also attracts success to us as well? One key ingredient is to increase the level of personal integrity from which we operate. Integrity is the foundation from which inner growth blossoms. All of us have a conscience, a sort of "inner knowing" or internal regulator, that tells us when we have been unjust, deceitful, or unethical. We can cover it up, rationalize it, or struggle to keep up a false front, but somewhere deep inside, we are aware of the contradiction. Any action, thought, or feeling that does not demonstrate integrity pulls us in ways that interfere with our ability to concentrate, be effective, and find pleasure in our lives.

When you find yourself in a situation that feels uncomfortable, simply refuse to participate. Excuse yourself quietly, or voice your concern. You will acquire greater self-esteem each time you resist the temptation to harm someone, to act in a negative way or manner that is not compatible with the person you know you are inside.

yourself and embrace all aspects of yourself, you have acquired integrity, which is the cornerstone of happiness and self-worth. It is essential for success on every level.

Believe in yourself, and do not be afraid to be the person you are right now. Make decisions that feel right for you, and do not worry about how others perceive you. In the end, if you act with integrity, you will acquire the respect of others. This is also crucial to success. Your own happiness is paramount. This does not mean giving up kindness; it means being kind to yourself first and foremost. When you feel good about yourself, it is that much easier to share your good feelings, which manifest themselves as daily acts of kindness. Kindness is a way of putting your new self-awareness into action by giving something of yourself. There are always opportunities in life for simple kindness. Show understanding and relate to others from your heart.

Adopt a sense of personal responsibility. People who experience high levels of success do what they know needs to be done, without complaining or being negative. Analyze your aspirations. Are your goals those that will satisfy and

fulfill you, or are they designed for someone else's approval? You will only achieve true happiness if you live your life in a way that makes you happy, every day. When you are independent and responsible, your sense of well-being is not contingent upon someone or something outside of yourself. Your very presence demonstrates a sense of self which is free from control or influence. You don't have trust issues with other people because you trust yourself to work through whatever you are facing. This enhances the integrity on which you choose to base your decisions. If you want love, be loving. If you want respect, be respectful. If you want honesty, be completely honest. If you want cooperation, be cooperative. Things will return to you the way you transmit them.

Depend on yourself. You can know what to do. All of us have periods where we feel victimized, underconfident, and unhappy, but these feelings come from allowing ourselves to be dependent on the outside world for approval. Only you can meet your own needs. The power to be what you want to be is within you, and when you have periods where you question this, remind yourself of your good qualities, the successes—however minor—that you have achieved in your life. Trust yourself and embrace self-responsibility.

We all have the innate ability to be whatever we want to be, to achieve whatever our hearts pull us toward. Act with integrity, both to yourself and to others, and you will make your journey. Self-belief engenders success because it involves celebrating and using the best of ourselves. When you experience doubt, use the power of positive thought to heal the wounds. Remind yourself with, "I can, I can do it."

Use your new-found confidence to communicate with others. Open your mind to change and to the beauty of the world around you. Recognize the beauty that is within you, and resolve to share it. You are no longer dependent upon others to define your self-worth. With self-awareness you will see a clear picture of yourself, and be able to express that self. You are strong, effective, emotionally honest, confident, open-minded, independent, decisive, intuitive, creative, intelligent, and communicative. You are a person that people like because you like yourself. You achieve your wildest dreams because you have found within yourself the tools with which to build them. You have the self-belief to see that the answers to everything life throws at you are within you. Most importantly, however, you are living your life as the person you really are. In that way, you are, and will always be, happy.

being SUCCESSFUL requires high self-esteem and self-respect

index

acknowledgments

The publishers would like to thank Theresa Reynolds for proofreading and The Indexing Specialists (UK) Limited for compiling the index.

Please note that the opinions and advice expressed in this book are intended as a guide only. The information given is not a substitute for medical advice. The publisher and authors accept no responsibility for any injury or loss sustained as a result of this book.